KELLY LEE CULBRETH

Nashville Travel Guide 2025-2026

The Ultimate Guide to Music City's Best Attractions, Music Venues, Outdoor Activities, Restaurants, Hotels, Events, and More

4C1
—Publishing—

First published by 401 Publishing 2025

Copyright © 2025 by Kelly Lee Culbreth

All rights reserved. No part of this publication may be reproduced, stored or transmitted in any form or by any means, electronic, mechanical, photocopying, recording, scanning, or otherwise without written permission from the publisher. It is illegal to copy this book, post it to a website, or distribute it by any other means without permission.

Kelly Lee Culbreth asserts the moral right to be identified as the author of this work.

Kelly Lee Culbreth has no responsibility for the persistence or accuracy of URLs for external or third-party Internet Websites referred to in this publication and does not guarantee that any content on such Websites is, or will remain, accurate or appropriate.

Designations used by companies to distinguish their products are often claimed as trademarks. All brand names and product names used in this book and on its cover are trade names, service marks, trademarks and registered trademarks of their respective owners. The publishers and the book are not associated with any product or vendor mentioned in this book. None of the companies referenced within the book have endorsed the book.

First edition

Don't just be a Dreamer... be a Doer too!

~ Kelly Lee Culbreth

Contents

101 Fun Facts About Nashville, TN   v
Introduction   vii

I   PLANNING & WHAT TO EXPECT

1   NASHVILLE'S CULTURE & LINGO   3
    Understanding Local Lingo and Slang   3
    Customs and Traditions   5
    Respectful Tips   6
2   PRE-TRIP PLANNING   7
    Planning Like a Pro   7
    Best Time to Visit Music City   9
    Weather   9
    Booking Your Stay   9
    💡Top 7 Must-Do Recommendations   10
    Restaurant Reservations   11
    Buying Tickets   12
3   TRANSPORTATION & NAVIGATING NASHVILLE   14
    Nashville Airport - BNA   14
    Ground Transportation: From the Airport to Downtown Nashville   16
    Cars, Traffic, and Parking   17
    Getting Around and About Downtown   18

II HOTELS, RESTAURANTS, & MUSIC VENUES BY NEIGHBORHOOD

4 DOWNTOWN NASHVILLE	23
Hotels	25
Music Venues	33
Restaurants	38
Printer's Alley	45
Fifth + Broadway – Mixed Use Assembly Hall	49
5 EAST NASHVILLE	50
Hotels	51
Music Venues	53
Restaurants	54
6 GERMANTOWN	59
Hotels	60
Music Venues	61
Restaurants	61
7 THE GULCH	65
Hotels	66
Music Venues	68
Restaurants	69
8 MIDTOWN, MUSIC ROW, & WEST END	75
Hotels	77
Music Venues	81
Restaurants	83
9 OPRYLAND HOTEL	91
Gaylord Opryland Resort & Convention Center	92
Music Venues Nearby	94

III ATTRACTIONS, CONCERT VENUES, & THE ARTS

10 LANDMARKS & MUST VISIT ATTRACTIONS	97
11 WORLD FAMOUS MUSIC VENUES	101
12 MUSEUMS & THE ARTS	103
Museums	103
Theaters	105
Art Galleries	106
Art Crawls	107
13 LARGE CONCERT & EVENT VENUES	109

IV BRUNCH, LIQUID GOLD, & SHOPPING

14 POPULAR BRUNCH SPOTS	115
Downtown	115
East Nashville	116
Germantown	117
The Gulch	117
Midtown, Music Row, and West End	118
15 LIQUID GOLD	119
Breweries and Distilleries	120
Vineyards & Wineries	124
16 SHOPPING	128
Boutiques & Fashion	128
Vintage & Local Finds	129
Music & Memorabilia	130
Markets & Artisan Goods	130
Shopping Malls & Outlets	131

V ANNUAL EVENTS & THINGS-TO-DO

17 FESTIVALS & ANNUAL EVENTS	135
Music Festivals & Concert Events	135
Cultural & Food Festivals	136
Seasonal & Holiday Events	138
Marathons & Races	138
18 UNIQUE THINGS-TO-DO	140
19 CHRISTMAS EVENTS & SHOWS	149

VI GREEN SPACES & SPORTS

20 PARKS & OPEN GREEN SPACES	155
Downtown	155
Surrounding Areas	157
21 SPORTS	159
Professional Sports	159
College Sports	160
Golf Courses	160
Public Sports Complexes	161
22 Share Your Experience	162
23 Conclusion	164
References	165
Also by Kelly Lee Culbreth	174

101 Fun Facts About Nashville, TN

Enhance your Nashville adventure with my other book, *101 Fun Facts About Nashville, TN*. This engaging book offers over **90 vibrant photographs and 101 captivating stories,** providing a comprehensive look into Nashville's iconic venues, museums, historical sites, and landmarks. Praised as a "fun and entertaining FULL-COLOR book," you can read about the city's rich history and dynamic live music scene.

This book serves as an inspiring prelude to your visit and makes a delightful gift and a charming coffee table addition to commemorate your time in Music City.

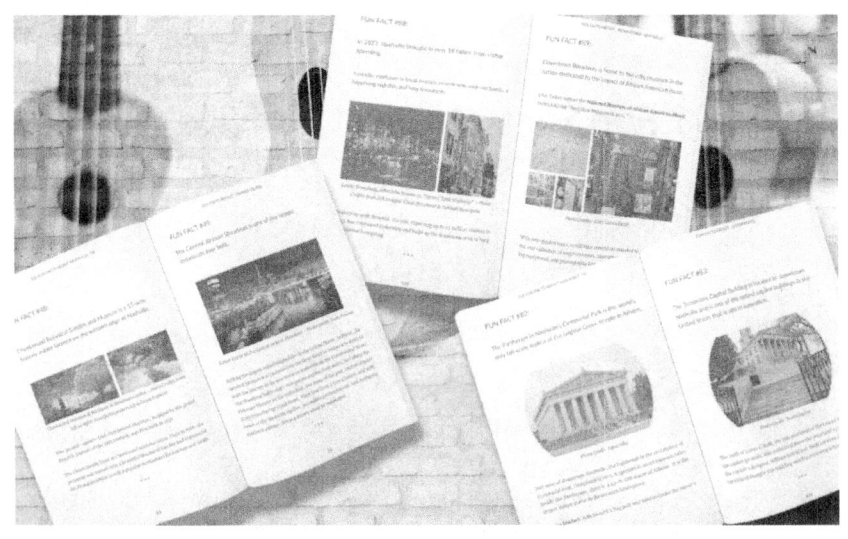

Introduction

Howdy, y'all! Whether you're a first-time visitor or returning for another trip, I'm thrilled to welcome you to Music City.

Nashville, a city rich in history, is more than just the capital of Tennessee. From its beginnings as a river port to becoming a vibrant cultural hub, Nashville is known for its world-renowned music scene.

As your guide, let me share my connection with this extraordinary city. I moved to Nashville in 1994 to attend Middle Tennessee State University. Over the past 30 years, I've witnessed Nashville's evolution into the dynamic city it is today. Here I am now—head over boots in love with this city. Now, I'm donning the hat of an author, sharing the stories and secrets that make Nashville tick.

In this guide, my goal is simple: to give you the most comprehensive insider's guide to this incredible city. I'll be your local companion, offering insights and tips only a Nashville enthusiast can provide. You will find everything about where to stay, eat, and play.

When packing for your trip, remember: in Nashville, there's no such thing as too much bling! Whether it's cowboy hats, boots, or rhinestones, make shopping for your Nashville adventure a part of the fun.

Want to unwind with the locals? I encourage you to explore the outer neighborhoods beyond the bustling downtown. There is an entire section dedicated to these popular neighborhoods. Because most locals don't go to Lower Broadway often - unless they are visiting Robert's Western World, a must-see we will discuss later.

With over 180 live music venues, Nashville is a symphony of sounds. Whether you're a night owl or a day drinker, the city has you covered. On Lower Broadway, honky tonks start playing live music as early as 10:00 am. From morning until night, you will not run out of things to do in Nashvegas!

Photo Credit: Garrett Hill - Lower Broadway on the 4th of July

Photo Credits from Left to Right: 12019 & Cesar G

*NOTE: If you'd like to suggest a business to be added to this travel guide or considered for future editions, we'd love to hear from you! Please email your recommendation to **401publishing@gmail.com** and include the business name, location, and any details that make it a great fit. Your input helps us create a more comprehensive and valuable resource for travelers.

I

PLANNING & WHAT TO EXPECT

1

NASHVILLE'S CULTURE & LINGO

Embracing their southern charm, Nashvillians have a language all their own. Words like "cathead" refer to a hearty biscuit, and "meat and three" signals a classic Southern dinner. Don't be surprised if you hear someone exclaiming "cattywampus" or inviting you to the "honky tonk highway"; these quirky expressions are part of the local lexicon.

Understanding Local Lingo and Slang

Nashville has its own unique slang and lingo that you might hear around town. Here are some of the most commonly used terms:

- **Hot Chicken**: A spicy fried chicken dish that originated in Nashville.
- **The Batman Building**: A local nickname for the AT&T Tower in downtown Nashville. It is currently the tallest building in Nashville.
- **Mother Church of Country Music**: The Ryman Auditorium is Nashville's most beloved concert venue.
- **The Preds**: A nickname for Nashville's beloved hockey team, The Predators.
- **Smashville:** Nashville hockey fans are known to be some of the

loudest in the league. The exuberant enthusiasm you will see at any hockey game has contributed to this nickname for Nashville.
- **Meat and Three:** A classic Southern dinner offering a choice of meat and three side dishes.
- **Cathead:** A giant biscuit, a delicious Southern comfort food.
- **Honky-Tonk Highway**: A stretch of Lower Broadway in downtown Nashville that is lined with honky-tonk bars and live music venues.
- **Lower Broad**: A shortened version of Lower Broadway, the main street in downtown Nashville.
- **The Gulch**: A trendy neighborhood in Nashville that is home to upscale restaurants, shops, and bars.
- **East Nashville**: A hip neighborhood in Nashville known for having an artsy vibe with an eclectic mix of bars and restaurants.
- **SoBro:** Stands for South of Broadway and is a popular downtown area with many attractions.
- **Bless your heart**: A phrase that can express sympathy, empathy, or even mild insult.
- **Fixin' to**: A phrase that means "about to" or "getting ready to" do something.
- **Y'all**: A contraction of "you all" that is used as a plural pronoun.
- **Cattywampus**: A word that means "askew" or "crooked."
- **Grits**: A Southern breakfast dish made from boiled cornmeal. (Try it with butter and sugar. That was my Dad's favorite way to eat grits.)
- **Holler**: A term that means "hollow" and describes a small valley or ravine.
- **Reckon**: A verb that means "to think" or "to suppose."
- **Yonder**: An adverb that means "over there" or "in the distance."
- **Pitch a fit**: To react with an outburst when angry or upset.
- **Hold your horses:** Be patient before acting.
- **Stompin' grounds:** Where you're from. Your turf. Your favorite hang.

- **NashVegas:** A term often associated with Nashville as a whole, but locals know this actually refers to Lower Broadway in all of its neon-lit, "why am I still up at 2 a.m." glory.

Customs and Traditions

When visiting Nashville, it's great to be aware of some customs and traditions to enhance your experience:

- **Live Music Everywhere:** Nashville is Music City, and you'll find live music in many places, from honky-tonks on Broadway to smaller venues in various neighborhoods. Embrace the local music scene and enjoy diverse genres. **Be sure to tip the musicians.**
- **Southern Hospitality:** Nashville is known for its warm hospitality. Don't be surprised if strangers strike up a friendly conversation.
- **Hot Chicken Tasting:** Trying hot chicken is a must. With various spice levels to choose from, Nashville's spicy fried chicken is a local specialty.
- **Predators Catfish Toss:** Attending a Nashville Predators hockey game? Witness the tradition of fans tossing catfish onto the ice for good luck since 2003. Getting giant catfish past security is not an easy task, and can carry a fine, but fans take the risk to keep the tradition alive.
- **Respect for History:** Nashville has a rich history, and there's a deep appreciation for it. Explore historic sites, like the Ryman Auditorium, and soak in the cultural heritage.
- **Sporting Events Enthusiasm:** Locals take their sports seriously, whether it's a Titans football game or a Predators Hockey game.

Respectful Tips

Observe Music Etiquette: Be mindful of the artists and fellow audience members when attending live music performances. Avoid excessive talking during performances to show respect for the musicians. **And always tip the musicians!** Many of them are full-time musicians working for tips only.

Tipping Culture: Tipping is customary in the United States. Be sure to tip service staff, including waitstaff, bartenders, musicians, and taxi drivers.

Respect Historic Sites: Nashville has many historical landmarks. Please treat them with respect, follow any guidelines, and appreciate the significance of these places.

Parking Courtesy: Follow parking regulations to avoid fines and avoid spaces reserved for residents or businesses. **To be safe, park your car in a parking garage for overnight stays.**

Be Mindful of Noise: Some neighborhoods have a residential vibe, so be mindful of your noise levels, especially in the evenings.

2

PRE-TRIP PLANNING

Preparing for your trip will ensure your stay is legendary. Planning is key. So, let's map out the perfect plan for your Nashville adventure!

Planning Like a Pro

VisitMusicCity.com is an excellent resource for travelers. This website provides information on upcoming events and must-see attractions. Whether you're interested in catching the hottest shows or attending one of the annual festivals, **VisitMusicCity.com** has a calendar of events that you can refer to for the dates of your trip.

QR Code for Visit Music City

Other great websites to check out for more event information, hotels, and resources are www.nashvilledowntown.com, www.NashvilleGo.com, or www.Nashvilleguru.com

If you want additional maps and resources after you arrive in Nashville, go to the **Nashville Convention & Visitors Corp's Visitor Center**. Located in the heart of downtown, this hub is your go-to spot for maps, brochures, and personalized recommendations.

Nashville Convention & Visitors Corp.
500 11th Ave N, Ste 650
Nashville, TN 37203
(800) 657-6910

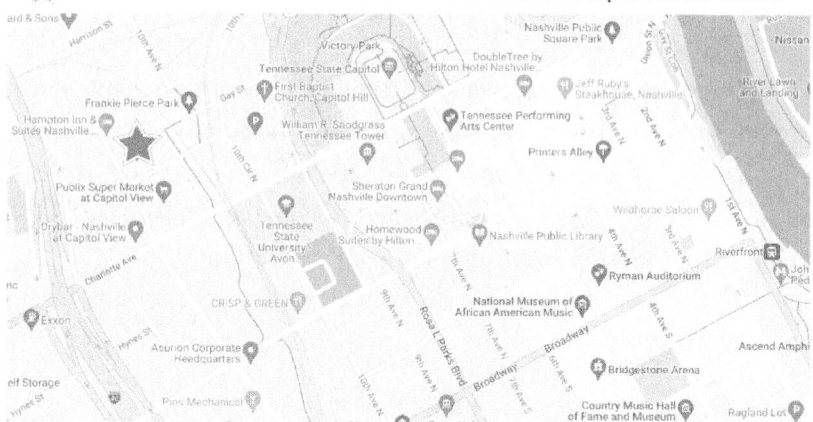

@2025 Google, Nashville Davidson County - (Downtown · Nashville, TN, USA, n.d.)

Best Time to Visit Music City

This is a trick question because anytime is a great time to visit Nashville! Music City welcomes visitors with open arms throughout the year, but the best time to see it in full swing is from April to October.

During these months, the warm weather sets the stage for a vibrant music scene and lively outdoor activities.

Weather

Nashville experiences all four seasons. The city wraps itself in a chilly embrace in winter while summer cranks up the heat. Spring and fall, the moderate maestros, offer cooler temps and a symphony of colors.

While packing your bags for Nashville, remember to check the weather. **WSMV.com** has spot-on forecasts.

But, ah, Nashville's weather can be unpredictable and full of surprises. So, stash a light jacket or umbrella in your suitcase in case the weather throws a plot twist.

Consider bringing your heavy outerwear in winter: a cozy coat, gloves, hats, and scarves to keep you snug during colder nights.

Booking Your Stay

When laying your head down in Nashville, you've got two leading players: hotels and Airbnb. Let's dive into the sweetest spots to catch those Zs:

- **Diverse Choices:** Hotels and Airbnbs top the charts, offering a range of choices for every traveler's taste.
- **Neighborhood Vibes:** Stay tuned for our upcoming chapters, where I will discuss top-notch hotels in each neighborhood. Pick your spot and book your stay accordingly.
- **Downtown Delights:** Fancy being in the heart of the action? Downtown serves up a mix of hotels and Airbnb's within a saunter's distance from all the must-see attractions.
- **Theme Time:** For a one-of-a-kind experience, explore one of the themed Airbnbs. With their quirky charm, these unique stays can make your trip memorable.
- **Location Matters:** Some accommodations might require a ride from Uber or Lyft to reach downtown or major attractions. Before hitting that "Book Now" button, check the map to ensure you're not in for a surprise commute.
- **Plan Ahead:** Whether you're team hotel or team Airbnb, decide what suits your vibe. Some hotspots book up fast. Don't procrastinate—get that reservation locked and loaded, especially if your heart is set on a specific spot.

💡Top 7 Must-Do Recommendations

1. **Listening Room Cafe** - It's an authentic "songwriter's round" dinner/brunch venue. **Backstage Nashville**, held at **3rd & Lindsley**, is similar and also highly recommended.
2. **The Parthenon in Centennial Park** - The only full-scale replica of the original Greek structure in the world!
3. **Honky Tonks on Lower Broadway-** TIP: Use the bathrooms and bartenders on the 2nd floor!
4. **Grand Ole Opry** - The world's longest-running radio show; even the commercials are still live!

5. **The Yee-Haw Brewing Company** - In the SoBro area of downtown. Family-friendly.
6. **Search StubHub** for the dates you're here and get tickets to a game or a concert: A show at the **Ryman or Opry**! **Predators, Sounds, and Titans games** are also fun!
7. **Printer's Alley** - This hidden gem is a 2-block alley full of world-class food and entertainment just a few steps from Broadway.

Restaurant Reservations

🍽 **A Feast for Every Palate:** Nashville's culinary landscape is as diverse as its music scene. From the homey charm of Southern meat and threes to the exquisite delights of 5-star restaurants, there's something for every taste bud in this city.

🔎 **Neighborhood Noshing:** Looking for the hottest spots in the neighborhood you are staying? Flip through the guide's chapters for restaurant recommendations by neighborhood.

🍴 **Fine Dining Reservations:** Do you want to experience Nashville's top-tier dining? Secure your spot **by making reservations 1-4 weeks in advance.** Some hotspots may have longer wait times, so plan accordingly.

NOTE: Reservations made in advance are recommended. Most dinner reservations can be made online. Some fine-dining restaurants have a dress code. Call ahead if you are unsure.

Buying Tickets

Here's your go-to guide for snagging must-have tickets.

✏️ **Early Bird Gets the Best Seats:** For major shows, venues, or sporting events, it's a Nashville golden rule – grab those tickets in advance! Events here tend to sell out fast, so secure your spot ahead of time for a stress-free experience.

🏛 **Museum Marvels and Tourist Treasures:** Good news for museum lovers and adventure seekers! Tickets for local museums and popular tourist hotspots are typically available on-site, and advance purchase may not be necessary. But a quick call ahead never hurts if you want to play it safe.

🗝 **Unlock Nashville's Charm with Discounts and Deals:** Discover vacation packages, discounted tickets, exclusive deals from local Nashville businesses, exciting giveaways, and more to help you save on your next trip to Music City at www.visitmusiccity.com.

QR Code for Discounts and Deals in Nashville, TN

🎟 **StubHub: Your Ticket Wonderland:** For games, shows, or concerts during your visit, go to **StubHub** for various dates and events. Find the perfect tickets hassle-free..

So, gear up, grab those tickets, and prepare to soak in Nashville's incredible entertainment!

Photo Credit: Larry Gibson

3

TRANSPORTATION & NAVIGATING NASHVILLE

Nashville Airport - BNA

Welcome to the Nashville International Airport, known as BNA. **https://flynashville.com/**

Description of BNA & Facilities

Here are some highlights:

- **Music Everywhere:** Waiting on your flight? Nashville's airport is filled with live music.
- **Dining Delights:** Hungry? BNA offers a range of dining options, from BBQ joints to coffee shops.
- **Shopping:** Forgot a souvenir? No problem. Explore the shops featuring local crafts, music memorabilia, and more.
- **Car Rental:** Need a ride? Rental car counters are located in the terminal, making exploring Nashville and its surroundings easy.

List of Airlines that Fly into Nashville

Nashville International Airport connects you to numerous destinations across the United States and beyond. Here's a list of airlines that operate at BNA:

AIRLINE:	FLIGHT INFORMATION:	RESERVATIONS:
Air Canada	888-422-7533	888-247-2262
Alaska Airlines	800-252-7522	800-2527522
Allegiant	702-505-8888	702-505-8888
American Airlines	800-223-5436	800-433-7300
British Airways	800-247-9297	800-247-9297
Contour Airlines	888-332-6686	888-332-6686
Delta Airlines	800-325-1999	800-221-1212
Frontier Airlines	801-401-9000	801-401-9000
JetBlue	800-538-2583	800-538-2583
Southwest	800-435-9792	800-435-9792
Spirit Airlines	855-728-3555	855-728-3555
Sun Country Airlines	800-800-6557	651-905-2737
United Airlines	800-824-6200	800-241-6522
Vacation Express	800-486-9777	800-486-9777
WestJet	888-937-8538	888-937-8538

Tips for a Smooth Experience at BNA

1. **Arrive Early:** Plan to arrive at least two hours before your domestic flight and three hours for international flights to allow time for security checks and any unexpected delays. BNA is a BUSY airport.
2. **Parking Options:** BNA offers various options, including short-term and long-term lots. For more details and pricing information, go to **https://flynashville.com/park-at-bna**.
3. **Security Check:** Have your ID and boarding pass ready. Follow the TSA guidelines for a hassle-free security check. For more information about BNA security screening, go to **https://flynashville.com/security-screening**

4. **Mobile Apps:** For real-time flight updates, terminal maps, and dining options, download the BNA app.

Ground Transportation: From the Airport to Downtown Nashville

Welcome to Nashville! After you've landed at the Nashville International Airport (BNA), there are several convenient options to get downtown.

1. Ride-Sharing Services

Uber and Lyft are two popular ride-sharing services that operate at BNA. You can quickly request a ride using their mobile apps. Look for designated pick-up areas outside the terminal.

💡**Tip:** Uber and Lyft offer reliable and convenient transportation. Compare prices to see which one offers the best price for your trip.

2. Rent a Car

Renting a car is an excellent option if you prefer the freedom to explore at your own pace. Nashville Airport hosts several reputable car rental companies right on-site, including:

- **Hertz:** www.hertz.com, Phone: (615) 275-2600
- **Enterprise:** www.enterprise.com, Phone: (615) 275-0011
- **Avis:** www.avis.com, Phone: (615) 361-1212
- **Budget:** www.budget.com, Phone: (615) 399-4777

Remember that while having your own wheels can be convenient, parking in downtown Nashville can be costly, and traffic can get heavy during peak hours. Check ahead of time if your accommodation offers parking options.

💡**Tip**: Some Airbnb locations may have free parking available.

3. Airport Shuttles to Your Hotel

Many hotels in Nashville provide airport shuttle services for their guests. Be sure to check with your hotel in advance to see if they offer this convenient option. Taking a hotel shuttle can save you time and hassle, especially during busy travel days and holidays when airport lines and traffic can be challenging. Most airport shuttles are FREE.

💡Travel Tip: Beat the Pick-Up Lines

If someone is picking you up at the airport during peak times, consider taking a shuttle to any nearby hotel instead of having them wait in the sometimes long pick-up lines at the airport. Your friends or family can pick you up from the hotel instead of the airport's arrival gate. This gets you out of the airport quickly, and your driver can avoid the airport traffic altogether.

So, whether you choose ride-sharing, renting a car, or using a hotel shuttle, you're all set to kick off your Nashville adventure.

Cars, Traffic, and Parking

You might be visiting Music City, but the traffic can be tricky. Here's what you need to know about cars, traffic, and parking in Nashville:

1. **Troubles:** During Nashville's peak times, especially during rush hours, you can expect the roads to be busy. Whether driving your

car into town or renting one at the airport, prepare for a few traffic jams.

2. **Timing is Key:** Plan your drives accordingly to avoid getting caught in heavy traffic. Heavy delays are common during morning and evening rush hours. Give yourself some extra time to enjoy your drive without the stress of being late.

3. **Parking Predicament:** Downtown Nashville has plenty of parking garages. However, convenience comes at a cost. Most parking facilities in the heart of the city require payment, so be sure to include parking expenses in your budget. Get quotes for car rentals and parking. Depending on the length of your trip, it may be cheaper to use Uber or Lyft instead.

4. **Accommodation Alternatives:** Some Airbnbs and hotels include parking in their packages, while others might charge separately or not offer it at all. Check with your lodging to know what to expect.

💡**Pro Tip—Pay for Peace of Mind:** Free parking downtown might sound enticing, but it's often not worth the risk. Paying for overnight parking in a secure garage is highly recommended to protect your car or rental from being towed or broken into. It's a small price to pay for peace of mind.

Getting Around and About Downtown

There are various transportation options you can use to explore Nashville. Here's how to navigate the downtown scene:

Walking: If you are staying downtown, walking is the way to go. Nashville's downtown area is incredibly pedestrian-friendly. You can visit Nashville's attractions, restaurants, and venues, soaking in the city as you wander.

Nashville B-Cycle Rental: To add a bit of adventure to your exploration, consider renting a bike. Nashville B-cycle provides a network of rentable bikes all over town. It's an excellent way to see the sights at your own pace. For more information and rental details, visit **https://bikethegreenway.net.**

Dash Scooters Rentals: For a fun and convenient way to zip around downtown, check out Dash Scooter Rentals. You can find more information and rental details on their website **https://dashscooterrental.com.**

Ride Share: Uber and Lyft are widely used in downtown Nashville.

💡**A helpful tip**: If you're staying in one of the outer neighborhoods, consider taking an Uber or Lyft to downtown. Enjoy the sites on foot and catch a ride back when you're ready. It's a practical and cost-effective choice.

Exploring Beyond Downtown: If you are staying in the heart of the city and plan to venture outside of downtown, ride-sharing services like Uber and Lyft are convenient. However, if you anticipate exploring many attractions outside the city center, renting a car might be more cost-effective, especially for longer drives of 15-30 minutes.

Public Transportation: For an economical way to visit the city's attractions, consider **WeGo Public Transit**. Their buses serve the city's tourist spots. For more information and schedules, visit **www.wegotransit.com.**

JoyRide: A fun and unique option, JoyRide offers street-legal golf cart taxis. These zippy vehicles can be a fun way to get around downtown. For details, check out their website at **https://joyrideus.com/nashville.**

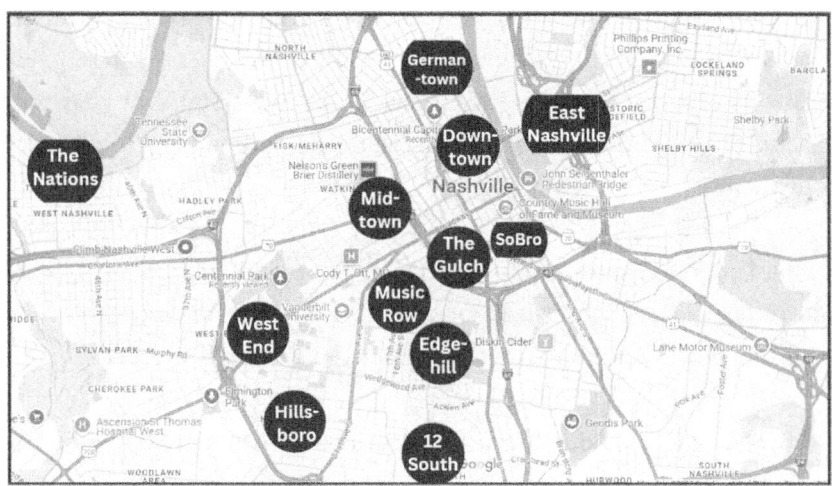

@2025 Google, Nashville Davidson County – (Downtown · Nashville, TN, USA, n.d.)

Photo Credit: Sean Pavone

II

HOTELS, RESTAURANTS, & MUSIC VENUES BY NEIGHBORHOOD

In this section, you can explore the various districts that make Nashville a vibrant tapestry of culture, music, and culinary delights.

HOTEL PRICE KEY PER NIGHT:
$ - $99 & under
$$ - $100-$199
$$$ - $200-$299
$$$$ - $300-$399
$$$$$ - $400+

Hotel prices fluctuate greatly during peak times.
Most fine-dining restaurants will require a reservation.

4

DOWNTOWN NASHVILLE

Downtown is known for: Partying, Live Music, and Amazing Restaurants.

Welcome to the heart of Music City, where the beats are lively, the food is delicious, and the energy is infectious. Downtown Nashville is a vibrant, bustling entertainment hub, and I'm here to guide you through its best offerings.

Lower Broadway - The Honky Tonk Highway

The heart of downtown Nashville is Lower Broadway, often referred to as the "Honky Tonk Highway." This iconic walkable strip is full of honky-tonks, bars, and live music venues. It's the place to go to experience Nashville's world-famous music scene.

SoBro - South of Broadway

Just south of Broadway, you'll find SoBro, a downtown neighborhood known for its modern vibe. It's the go-to spot for "all things new and exciting" in downtown Nashville, with some of the most popular attractions in this area.

Printers Alley

Printer's Alley, located between Third and Fourth Avenues in downtown Nashville, is a historic district famous for its nightlife and cultural heritage. This two-block area has a distinct identity and features an array of hotels, restaurants, bars, and music venues.

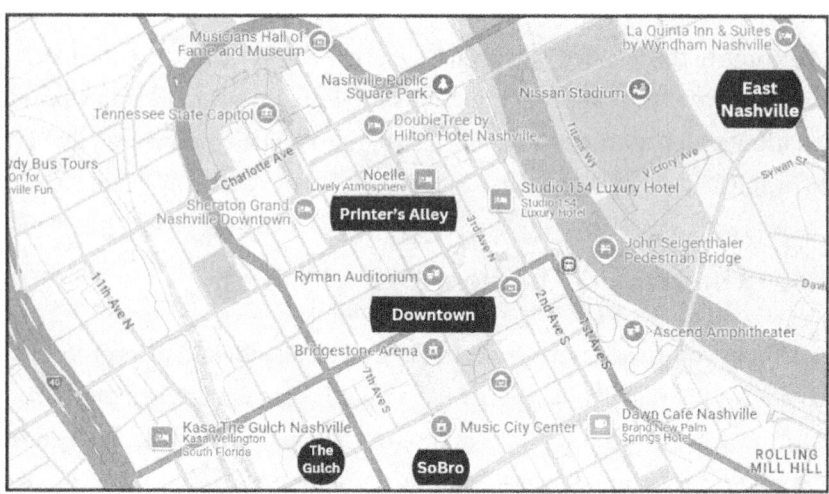

@2025 Google, Nashville Davidson County - (Downtown · Nashville, TN, USA, n.d.)

Hotels

Downtown has a wide array of options for your overnight trip. There are hotels, condos, and unique lofts. Here are some of the most popular and unique options in the downtown area:

1 Hotel Nashville - 710 Demonbreun Street - (615) 510-0400: Sustainable luxury located in the heart of downtown. This hotel boasts an ivy-covered exterior with over 56,000 individual plants and a great rooftop bar. www.1hotels.com/nashville

- Pets: Allowed with no additional fee, pet amenities available
- Price Range: $$$$-$$$$$

506 Lofts Nashville - 506 Church Street - (615) 861-9535: This place is unique and artsy, and you get a lot for your money. These lofts offer a distinctive blend of industrial design and comfortable furnishings, creating a welcoming atmosphere for guests. Located blocks from **Printer's Alley.** www.506lofts.com

- Pets: Not allowed
- Price Range: $$-$$$

Bobby Hotel - 230 4th Ave N - (615) 782-7100: A charming boutique hotel in downtown's heart near **Printer's Alley**. It features a popular **rooftop bar.** One of the hotel's highlights is the Rooftop Lounge, which hosts a vintage winter pop-up experience. Guests can rent private campfire igloos and enjoy a vintage holiday lounge while viewing Nashville's skyline. https://bobbyhotel.com/

- Pets: Allowed with no additional fee - pet amenities available

- Price Range: $$-$$$

Cambria Hotel Nashville Downtown - 118 8th Ave S - (615) 515-5800: Located in the SoBro downtown area, this hotel boasts a contemporary design with chic rock-n-roll décor and modern furnishings. Relax and unwind at the **rooftop pool**, where you can take in panoramic views of the city. www.cambrianashville.com

- Pets: Not Allowed
- Price Range: $$

DoubleTree by Hilton Hotel Nashville Downtown - 315 4th Avenue N - (615) 244-8200: This hotel provides guests with full-service amenities to ensure a pleasant stay. It is only a 10-minute walk from Broadway and the renowned Ryman Auditorium. DoubleTree Nashville Downtown

- Pet Policy: Allowed with a one-time $75 fee
- Price Range: $$

Dream Nashville - 210 4th Avenue N - (615) 622-0600: This luxurious and art-deco-inspired boutique hotel is located near **Printer's Alley**. www.dreamhotels.com/nashville

- Pets: Allowed with no additional fee
- Price Range: $$-$$$

Fairlane Hotel Nashville - 401 Union Street - (615) 988-8511: A retro-modern downtown boutique hotel offering a unique 70's style experience. Enjoy a **rooftop bar** with views of the Nashville skyline and within walking distance of popular downtown attractions. www.fairlanehotel.com

- Pets: Allowed with a one-time $75 fee
- Price Range: $$-$$$

Four Seasons Hotel Nashville - 100 Demonbreun Street - (615) 610-5001: The Four Seasons Hotel enjoys a prime location in the SoBro neighborhood. It's conveniently close to the city's major attractions. Guests can relax by the **rooftop pool** while enjoying views of the Nashville skyline. The Four Seasons is known for its world-class service and attention to detail. www.fourseasons.com/nashville

- Pets: Allowed with no additional fee
- Price Range: $$$$$+

Grand Hyatt Hotel - 1000 Broadway - (615) 622-1234: Nestled on the western edge of downtown, this hotel is also within walking distance of the Gulch and the Midtown district. The hotel boasts exceptional dining options, fitness facilities, and a **rooftop bar** with city views. www.hyatt.com/Nashville

- Pets: Allowed with a one-time $100 fee
- Price: $$-$$$

Hilton Nashville Downtown - 121 4th Ave S - (615) 620-1000: Located in the SoBro area, the Hilton provides easy access to Nashville's iconic attractions, including the Country Music Hall of Fame and Museum, Bridgestone Arena, and the vibrant Broadway entertainment district. Guests can unwind at the **rooftop pool** with views of the Nashville skyline. Hilton Nashville Downtown

- Pets: Allowed with a one-time $50 fee.
- Price Range: $$-$$$

Holiday Inn Express Nashville Downtown - 920 Broadway - (615) 244-0150: This modern hotel offers comfortable accommodations and excellent amenities, making it an ideal choice for leisure and business travelers. This hotel is within walking distance of downtown's most popular attractions. Holiday Inn Express - Nashville Downtown

- Pets: Not allowed
- Price Range: $-$$

Holston House Nashville by Hyatt - 118 7th Ave N - (615) 392-1234: This unique boutique hotel is part of the Unbound Collection by Hyatt. It holds the prestigious AAA 4-Diamond rating and is adjacent to the iconic Ryman Auditorium. The hotel is known for its modern amenities, including a **rooftop pool**. Holston House Hotel is also home to the Tenn on Top restaurant and the Heirloom **Rooftop bar** with stunning views of the Nashville skyline. Holston House Nashville

- Pets: Allowed with no additional fee
- Price: $$$

Homewood Suites by Hilton - Nashville - 706 Church Street - (615) 742-5550: Located in the historic downtown district. This all-suite hotel offers a comfortable and home-like atmosphere and an indoor pool. Each suite features a fully equipped kitchen. Nashville Homewood Suite by Hilton

- Pets: Allowed with a one-time $75 fee
- Price Range: $-$$

Hotel Indigo Nashville - The Countrypolitan - 315 Union Street - (615) 891-6000: A unique and vibrant downtown hotel located directly in the historic **Printers Alley**. Hotel Indigo Nashville

- Pets: Allowed with a one-time $75 fee
- Price: $$-$$$

Margaritaville Hotel Nashville - 425 5th Ave S - (615) 896-9300: Located in the SoBro neighborhood, the laid-back lifestyle of singer Jimmy Buffett inspired this vibrant hotel. Guests can enjoy amenities such as a **rooftop pool** with a sundeck and live entertainment. https://www.margaritavilleresorts.com/margaritaville-hotel-nashville

- Pets: Allowed with a one-time $100 fee
- Price: $$$-$$$$

Noelle Nashville, a Tribute Portfolio Hotel - 200 4th Ave N - (615) 649-5000: Located in **Printer's Alley**, this historic hotel has been reimagined with 224 luxury rooms and pays homage to its Art Deco roots. The Noelle Hotel features a Hidden Bar, a well-kept secret within the hotel, where you can enjoy classic European cocktails and unexpected delights. www.noelle-nashville.com

- Pets: Allowed with a one-time $100 fee
- Price: $$-$$$

Omni Nashville Hotel - 250 Rep. John Lewis Way South - (615) 782-5300: Situated in the SoBro area, the hotel is conveniently **connected to the Country Music Hall of Fame and Museum**. With over 80,000 square feet of flexible event space, including a **rooftop terrace and pool**, the hotel is ideal for weddings, conferences, and special occasions. Omni Nashville Hotel

- Pets: Allowed with a one-time $125 fee
- Price Range: $$-$$$$

Renaissance Nashville Hotel - 611 Commerce Street - (615) 255-8400: This contemporary, elegant hotel is **connected to the Nashville Convention Center** and is conveniently situated near many of Nashville's top attractions, including the Country Music Hall of Fame and Bridgestone Arena. Renaissance Nashville Hotel

- Pets: Allowed for a fee of $50/night or $150 max
- Price Range: $$$

Sheraton Grand Nashville Downtown - 623 Union Street - (615) 259-2000: An upscale and modern downtown hotel with stunning views. This stylish hotel offers luxury and comfort for both business and leisure travelers. They offer a complimentary Golf Cart Shuttle service to Broadway. Sheraton Grand Nashville Downtown

- Pets: Allowed with no additional fee - pet amenities available
- Price Range: $$-$$$

Sonder - Apartment Rentals: Sonder offers a range of apartment rentals designed for **short-term and extended stays**. From studios to 4-bedroom apartments, these accommodations are thoughtfully furnished and provide travelers with a comfortable and homey environment. **Some notable Sonder properties in Nashville are in the following neighborhoods:** Downtown Nashville, Hillsboro Village, Germantown, East Nashville, SoBro, Midtown, Music Row, West End, and Wedgewood Houston. www.sonder.com

Studio 154 Luxury Hotel - 154 2nd Ave - (615) 891-0154: A pioneering boutique hotel in the heart of downtown along the Cumberland River on 2nd Ave. The hotel's **SKYDECK** is a highlight, offering panoramic views of the city skyline. A 1,700-square-foot, two-story modern suite sleeps up to 12 guests for larger parties. www.studio154nashville.com

- Pets: Not allowed
- Price Range: $$-$$$$

The Bankers Alley Hotel Nashville, Tapestry Collection by Hilton - 221 2nd Ave - 615-610-6400: A combination of contemporary art museum and boutique hotel featuring museum-worthy art, delicious food, and cocktails at Gray and Dudley. The Bankers Alley Hotel Nashville

- Pets: Allowed with a $75 fee
- Price Range: $$-$$$

The Capitol Hotel Downtown, Ascend Hotel Collection - 711 Union Street - (615) 242-4311: Part of the Ascend Hotel Collection, this is a chic and welcoming boutique hotel located in the heart of downtown. It offers spacious rooms with modern comforts. The Capitol Hotel Downtown

- Pets: Not allowed
- Price: $-$$

The Hermitage Hotel - 231 6th Ave N - (888) 888-9414: Established in 1910, The Hermitage is a true Nashville icon known for its timeless elegance and Southern charm. Near the Tennessee Performing Arts Center, it has been a beacon of luxury for over a century. Its grand lobby, adorned with marble floors and crystal chandeliers, exudes opulence. The Hermitage offers a range of luxurious accommodations, from spacious rooms to lavish suites. www.thehermitagehotel.com

- Pets: Allowed with a fee - pet amenities available
- Price: $$$$-$$$$$

The Joseph, a Luxury Collection Hotel - 401 Korean Veterans Blvd - (615) 248-1990: The Joseph is a testament to Nashville's thriving arts scene. Guests will be immersed in a visually stunning environment from the moment they arrive. The Joseph is situated in the SoBro neighborhood and provides easy access to Nashville's renowned arts and entertainment venues. Broadway and downtown attractions are within close reach. www.thejosephnashville.com

- Pets: Allowed with a one-time fee of $150
- Price Range: $$$$-$$$$$

The Union Station Nashville Yards - 1001 Broadway - (615) 726-1001: This historic and luxurious hotel is located downtown and within walking distance of The Gulch and Midtown districts. Established in 1900, this former train terminal has become a signature historic hotel for modern-day travelers. www.unionstationhotelnashville.com

- Pets: Allowed with a one-time fee of $100
- Price Range: $$$$

The Westin Nashville - 807 Clark Place - (615) 248-2800: This luxury hotel offers skyline views from the **rooftop pool and lounge** across the street from the Music City Center in the SoBro area. The Westin Nashville is just steps away from popular attractions like the Country Music Hall of Fame and Museum and the Broadway entertainment district. The Westin Nashville

- Pets: Allowed for a fee of $50/night or a max of $150
- Price Range: $$$$

* * *

Music Venues

Open seven days a week, every honky tonk on Broadway has its own unique flavor and history. Getting the most out of a night on Broadway isn't just about **hopping from one honky tonk to another**; it's about immersing yourself in the energy and the music. So, don't be afraid to interact with the musicians. They are known for being friendly!

***Make sure to tip the musicians! ***

FREE: All the music venues on Lower Broadway are free. So you can spend an evening or two checking out all the live music venues lining the "Honky Tonk Highway" known as Lower Broadway.

TIP #1: The honky tonks downtown get overly crowded on the weekend, and there can be waits to get in. Go during the weekdays to avoid the larger crowds. Even better: go during the day. The bands start playing as early as 10:00 am.

TIP #2: Don't forget about the 2nd floor! Go upstairs to order your drinks and use the bathroom to avoid the longer lines on the 1st floor!

Photo Credits: Mana5280

Popular Honky Tonks & Music Venues on Lower Broadway and Downtown:

*** Robert's Western World - 416 Broadway: A beloved local gem on Lower Broadway, famous for its traditional country music. **Voted *Nashville Scene*'s Local Favorite Honky Tonk for the last 8 years in a row!** (*Robert's Western World (n.d.) | 2023*) *** https://robertswesternworld.com/

3rd & Lindsley - 818 3rd Ave S: A few blocks from downtown, this live music venue hosts local, regional, and national artists and bands - with full food and drinks. Make sure to check out their **calendar of events**: www.3rdandlindsley.com

Acme Feed & Seed - 101 Broadway: A venue with multiple levels and features creative cuisine, cocktails & live music, plus a large rooftop patio overlooking the Cumberland River and Lower Broadway. www.acmefeedandseed.com/

AJs Good Time Bar - 421 Broadway: is Alan Jackson's urban honky-tonk. It offers three floors, live country music & a rooftop bar. www.ajsgoodtimebar.com/

Casa Rosa - 308 Broadway: Owned by Miranda Lambert, Casa Rosa is a Tex-Mex and cantina-style restaurant and entertainment venue on Broadway. There are four floors with great food and live music. https://casarosanashville.com/

Chief's on Broadway - 200 Broadway: Eric Church's Music Venue has six floors that include live music, a bar, and a rooftop BBQ joint. www.chiefsonbroadway.com/

City Winery - 609 Lafayette St: Restaurant & Wine Bar with a selection of tap wine options. Enjoy a great dinner and live music and shows. Make sure to check out their **calendar of events:** www.citywinery.com/nashville

Dierks Bentley's Whiskey Row - 400 Broadway: A modern American gastropub and live music venue with a rooftop lounge. https://dierkswhiskeyrow.com/nashville-tn/

Friends in Low Places Bar & Honky-Tonk - 411 Broadway: A 4-story bar, restaurant, and live music venue. www.friendsbarnashville.com/

Honky Tonk Central - 329 Broadway: A very popular 3-story honky tonk featuring pub eats and live music on every floor. www.honkytonkcentral.com/

Jason Aldean's Kitchen + Rooftop bar - 307 Broadway: A southern eatery with four levels of live music and a rooftop bar. https://jasonald

eansbar.com/

Jelly Roll's Goodnight Nashville - 209 Broadway: NOW OPEN! A four-story venue that features a mix of Southern comfort food, live music, and unique decor. Highlights include a first floor with a full bar and live performances, a second floor dedicated to Jelly Roll's wife, Bunnie Xo, with DJ sets, and a cozy third floor, "Buddy's Back Room," honoring his late father. The rooftop offers city views, a rotating skull chandelier, and a DJ area. https://goodnightnashville.com/

Kid Rock's Big Ass Honky Tonk Rock N' Roll Steakhouse - 221 Broadway: Offering live music on multiple levels of a three-story building, Kid Rock's Rock N' Roll Steakhouse is known for being one of Nashville's biggest and most energetic honky-tonk bars. www.kidrockshonkytonkandsteakhouse.com/

Lainey Wilson's Bell Bottoms Up - 120 3rd Ave S: Brand new 27,000 square-foot, 3-story entertainment venue with a rooftop dance floor. https://bellbottomsupbar.com/

Laylas Honky Tonk - 418 Broadway: A live bluegrass and country music venue that is lined with Vintage license plates on the ceiling of this lively, intimate bar. www.laylasnashville.com/

Legends Corner - 428 Broadway: A popular honky tonk with a strong presence in the Nashville music scene with locals and tourists. It offers a classic dive bar experience. www.legendscorner.com/

Listening Room Cafe - 618 4th Ave S: An intimate venue for singer-songwriters and acoustic performances. A must-visit for music enthusiasts. Make sure to check out their **calendar of events:** www.listeningr

oomcafe.com/nashville-shows

Luke's 32 Bridge - 301 Broadway: Luke Bryan's 32 Bridge offers dining and cocktails, three stages, 7 bars, and a roof-top patio inside this 6-floor entertainment venue. https://lukes32bridge.com/

Nashville Crossroads - 419 Broadway: Features classic country music and southern rock-n-roll. https://nashvilledowntown.com/go/nashville-crossroads

Ole Red - 300 Broadway: Inspired by Blake Shelton's chart-topping hit, "Ol' Red," this venue combines various elements, making it a unique destination. Ole Red serves as a restaurant, live music venue, and retail space. https://olered.com/nashville/

Rippy's Honky Tonk - 429 Broadway: Located across the street from Bridgestone arena, this is a popular venue to visit before and after events at Bridgestone. There are several levels and a rooftop with live music on every floor. www.rippyshonkytonk.com/

The Stage - 412 Broadway: A popular honky-tonk featuring live country bands & a dance floor by a large mural depicting music icons. Has a rooftop bar. www.thestageonbroadway.com/

Tin Roof - 316 Broadway: Multi-level bar and restaurant with live music. https://tinroofbroadway.com/

Tootsies Orchard Lounge - 422 Broadway: A historical watering hole across the alley from The Ryman Auditorium. Multiple levels with a rooftop bar. www.tootsies.net/

Whiskey Bent Saloon – 306 Broadway: A vibrant, rustic tavern with mounted animal heads, live music, beer, and cocktails. www.whiskeybentsaloon.com/

Karaoke Locations:

- **AJs Good Time Bar – 421 Broadway:** Karaoke begins at 7:00 pm on the 3rd floor every day.
- **Lonnie's Western Room Karaoke Bar – 308 Church Street:** Open Thursday, Friday, Saturday, and Sunday from 6 pm to close.
- **Ms. Kelli's Karaoke Bar – 207 Printer's Alley:** Doors open at 7:00 pm every night.
- **Wanna B's Karaoke Bar – 305 Broadway:** Located inside Tequila Cowboys, Wanna B's is open Thursday, Friday, Saturday, and Sunday from 2 pm to close.
- **Wild Beaver Saloon Karaoke Bar – 212 Commerce Street:** Doors open at 5:00 pm every night except Saturdays, which open at 1:00 pm.

* * *

Restaurants

With a thriving culinary scene, Nashville has an array of restaurants to satisfy every palate. While there are too many exceptional restaurants to mention them all, I've compiled a list of some of the city's most popular and beloved dining establishments. Whether you're in the mood for Southern comfort food, international cuisine, or fine dining experiences, Nashville has it all.

💡**TIP:** Call ahead to make reservations. Many fine dining restaurants listed below will require a reservation in advance.

Fine Dining:

Cafe Intermezzo - 205 Demonbreun Street - (615) 840-7933: A family-owned dining destination known for its European-inspired atmosphere and extensive dessert and coffee offerings. It's an excellent destination for those looking to experience a taste of Europe in the heart of Music City. **European-style Restaurant - Menu:** www.cafeintermezzo.com/location-nashville-tn -

Eddie V's Prime Seafood - 590 Broadway - (615) 238-2359: An elegant fine-dining chain known for its seafood & steaks, plus a cocktail lounge featuring live jazz. **Seafood & Steak - Menu:** www.eddiev.com/menu

Etch - 303 Demonbreun St - (615) 522-0685: A globally-inspired restaurant by award-winning chef Deb Paquette with an open-kitchen setting for eclectic, upscale dining, plus a rich cocktail & wine list. **Eclectic Restaurant - Menu:** www.etchrestaurant.com/nashville/menu/

Gannons Nashville - 170 4th Ave N - (615) 920-6792: A restaurant known for its Oysters & Cocktail Bar. Great location for live jazz and an unmatched dinner experience! **American Restaurant - Menu:** www.gannonsnashville.com/

House of Cards - 119 3rd Ave S - (615) 730-8326: Magic show and dinner. A one-of-a-kind dining and entertainment experience located underground in a 10,000-square-foot space. *There is a dress code* - check their website for more information. **21 & up only. American**

Restaurant & Magic Show - Menu: www.hocnashville.com/menu

Husk - 37 Rutledge St - (615) 256-6565: Located inside a historic mansion – just a few blocks south of Broadway – Executive Chef Ben Norton leads Husk. The restaurant uses locally sourced, seasonal ingredients to create dishes that showcase the region's flavors. **Southern Restaurant - Menu:** www.husknashville.com/food/menu/

Jeff Ruby's Steakhouse - 300 4th Ave N - (615) 434-4300: A top-notch dining destination for those seeking an elevated steakhouse experience. Has prime steaks, exquisite sushi, fresh seafood, and award-winning sides. **Steakhouse - Menu:** www.jeffruby.com/nashville/menus

Pinewood Social - 33 Peabody St - (615) 751-8111: Trendy hangout in an industrial-chic space featuring New American cuisine, cocktails & bowling. **It's a restaurant, coffee shop, workspace, outdoor hangout, and bowling alley.** There are also small swimming pools, shuffleboard, and Bocce. The restaurant's culinary offerings are also exceptional. **They also offer free parking!** New American Restaurant - Menu: www.pinewoodsocial.com/consume

The Farm House Restaurant & Bar - 210 Almond St - (615) 522-0688: Led by Chef Trey Cioccia, this restaurant offers Southern-inspired cuisine that celebrates locally sourced ingredients with a menu that features seasonal dishes with a commitment to farm-to-table principles. **American Restaurant - Menu:** www.thefarmhousetn.com

The Hampton Social - 201 1st Ave S - (615) 622-7772: Breezy hangout with stylish, nautical surroundings serving seafood & beach-themed cocktails. Known for its rooftop experience, the menu at Hampton Social features coastal cuisine, hand-crafted cocktails, and their signature

Rosé wine. **American Restaurant - Menu:** www.thehamptonsocial.com/nashville-menu

The Southern Steak & Oyster - 150 3rd Ave S - (615) 636-2626: Located in the SoBro district, The Southern is nestled in Nashville's first LEED-certified high-rise, the restaurant showcases a commitment to sustainability by featuring locally grown produce in its menu offerings. **Southern Inspired Steak & Oyster House - Menu:** thesouthernnashville.com/menu

The Twelve-Thirty Club - 550 Broadway - Reservations done online only: Justin Timberlake is part owner of this swanky, upscale venue offering modern regional cuisine, a bar, live music & rooftop dining. Located inside 5th + Broadway Assembly Hall, the Twelve-Thirty Club has become a renowned restaurant and bar known for offering an unforgettable Nashville experience. **American Restaurant - Menu:** www.thetwelvethirtyclub.com

Yolan - 403 4th Ave S - (615) 231-0405: An authentic experience of Italian cuisine done right, specializing in avant-garde entrees, plus an impressive wine list. Chef di Cucina Joey Fecci leads the culinary team, overseeing menu creation and research, ensuring Yolan's offerings are seasonally inspired and regionally authentic to Italy. Inside The Joseph Luxury Hotel. - **Italian - Menu:** www.yolannashville.com/menus

Casual Dining:

- Most honky tonks on Lower Broadway will offer bar food
- **Acme Feed & Seed -** 101 Broadway: Elevated Southern food & cocktails
- **Bakersfield Tacos & Tequilla -** 201 3rd Ave South

- **Batter's Box** - 43 Hermitage Ave: A local watering hole that allows smoking
- **Cafe Intermezzo** - 205 Demonbreun Street: - European-inspired dishes
- **Fifth + Broadway** - 5036 Broadway: 20+ casual dining options to pick from
- **Frothy Monkey** - 235 Rep John Lewis Way N
- **Hattie B's Hot Chicken** - 5069 Broadway: located inside the 5th + Broadway Assembly Hall.
- **Jack's BBQ** - 416 Broadway
- **Johnny Cash's Bar & BBQ** - 121 3rd Ave South
- **Martin's BBQ**- 410 4th Ave South: Has a beer garden with darts, shuffleboard, and ping pong
- **Merchants** - 401 Broadway: Casual bistro downstairs & formal dining upstairs
- **Puckett's Grocery & Restaurant** - 500 Church Street: Southern bar & grill
- **Rippy's Honky Tonk** - 429 Broadway: American Barfood
- **The Diner** - 200 3rd Ave South: 6 floors of casual and upscale dining
- **The Goat - SoBro** - 211 Elm Street
- **The Pancake Pantry** - 220 Molloy St
- **The Stillery** - 113 2nd Ave North - Burgers, pizza, and hot chicken
- **Yee-Haw Brewing Co.** - 423 6th Ave South: Brewery and beer hall, moonshine, live music and bar bites

Sports Bars:

- **Barlines at the Omni:** 250 Rep. John Lewis Way South
- **Barstool - Nashville:** 123 2nd Ave South
- **Batter's Box:** 43 Hermitage Ave (a local watering hole that allows smoking)

- **Broadway Brewhouse:** 317 Broadway
- **Corner Pub - Downtown:** 151 5th Ave North
- **Draft Kings Sports and Social:** 128 2nd Ave North
- **Fleet Street Pub:** 207 Printers Alley
- **Jonathans Grille:** 717 3rd Ave North
- **Loser's Bar & Grill:** 111 4th Ave South
- **Lucky Bastard Saloon:** 408 Broadway
- **Rippy's Honky Tonk:** 429 Broadway
- **Teddy's Tavern** - 104 Rep. John Lewis Way South: Located across from Bridgestone Arena in one of the oldest buildings downtown. This historic spot is great to visit before or after a game, concert, or event.
- **The Stillery:** 113 2nd Ave North

Rooftop Bars:

- Many of the bars and honky tonks on Broadway will have a rooftop bar.
- **Bobby Hotel Rooftop Lounge:** 230 4th Ave North
- **Harriet's Rooftop:** 710 Demonbreun - 18th floor of 1 Hotel Nashville
- **Lou/Na:** 1000 Broadway
- **Nashville Underground:** 105 Broadway - only double-decker rooftop on Broadway
- **Rare Bird:** 200 4th Ave North
- **The Overlook Rooftop Bar & Grill:** 125 7th Ave South
- **The Twelve-Thirty Club:** 550 Broadway
- **The Valentine:** 312 Broadway
- **Zeppelin Rooftop Bar & Lounge:** 505 3rd Ave North

Nightclubs:

- **Blueprint Underground Cocktail Club:** 156 Printers Alley
- **Brooklyn Bowl:** 925 3rd Ave N
- **Category 10:** 120 2nd Ave N
- **Club One21:** 121 3rd Ave S
- **Dirty Little Secret:** 210 Printers Alley
- **La Danse Bar:** 142 Rosa L Parks Blvd
- **Night We Met:** 114 12th Ave N
- **Play Dance Bar (Midtown):** 1519 Church St. Gay Night Club
- **Skull's Rainbow Room:** 222 Printers Alley
- **Skydeck on Broadway:** 5055 Broadway Place (rooftop of Assembly Food Hall within the Fifth + Broadway development)

Desserts:

- **Cafe Intermezzo:** 205 Demonbreun Street
- **Corner Bakery Cafe:** 308 4th Ave South
- **Cotton & Snow:** 5055 Broadway (inside Fifth + Broadway)
- **D'Andrews Bakery & Cafe:** 555 Church St
- **Donut Distillery:** 5055 Broadway (inside Fifth + Broadway)
- **Goo Goo Chocolate Co:** 116 3rd Ave South
- **Hattie Jane's Creamery:** 5055 Broadway (inside Fifth + Broadway)
- **Jeni's Splendid Ice Creams:** 5054 Broadway (inside Fifth + Broadway)
- **Layer Cake:** 127 3rd Ave South
- **Legendairy Milkshake Bar:** 171 3rd Ave North
- **Le Macaron Nashville:** 5006 Broadway (inside Fifth + Broadway)
- **Mattheessen's Ice Cream:** 123 2nd Ave North
- **Mike's Ice Cream:** 129 2nd Ave North
- **Parlor Doughnuts:** 506 Rep. John Lewis Way S

- **Savannah Candy Kitchen:** 310 Broadway
- **Tempered Fine Chocolates:** 1201 5th Ave North, Suite 103

Coffee:

- **Bongo Java:** 364 Rep. John Lewis Way S
- **Cafe at Bobby:** 230 4th Ave North
- **Cafe Intermezzo:** 205 Demonbreun Street
- **Crema Coffee Roasters:** 15 Hermitage Ave
- **D'Andrews Bakery & Cafe:** 555 Church Street
- **Drug Store Coffee:** 200 4th Ave North
- **Elegy Coffee Downtown:** 150 4th Ave North
- **E+ROSE Wellness Bodega at 505 Nashville:** 501 Church Street
- **Frothy Monkey:** 235 Rep. John Lewis Way North
- **Moonshot Coffee Bar:** 300 Gay Street
- **Pinewood Social Coffee Bar:** 33 Peabody Street
- **PJ's Coffee:** 414 Union Street
- **Prickly Pear Coffee Co:** 333 Commerce Street

* * *

Printer's Alley

Tucked away from the bustling Lower Broadway area, **Printer's Alley** in downtown Nashville is a hidden treasure steeped in history and known for its vibrant nightlife.

Location: The Alley entrance is on Church Street between 3rd Ave & 4th Ave.

Here's a glimpse into what you can discover in this historic alleyway:

- **Historic Significance**: Printer's Alley has a rich history dating back to the 19th century when it housed numerous printing shops. Over the years, it evolved into a hub for music and entertainment.
- **Late-Night Entertainment**: Printer's Alley is famous for its late-night jazz, blues, and karaoke bars. The Alley comes alive with live music after the sun sets, making it a must-visit destination for night owls and music lovers.
- **Diverse Music Scene**: You can experience a diverse music scene in Printer's Alley, with various venues offering everything from classic jazz to modern blues and rock.
- **Unique Atmosphere**: The alley's intimate and cozy ambiance adds to its charm. It's a great place to unwind and listen to live music.
- **Local Landmarks**: Printer's Alley has several historic landmarks, including the famous **Skull's Rainbow Room**, which has a fascinating history as a speakeasy during the Prohibition era.
- **Karaoke and Nightlife**: Many bars offer karaoke nights, where you can showcase your singing talents on stage.
- **Hidden Gem**: Tucked away from the bustling streets of downtown Nashville, Printer's Alley offers a unique and somewhat secretive experience. You can escape the mainstream and discover the city's authentic soul here.

Restaurants in Printer's Alley:

Black Rabbit - 218 3rd Ave N - (615) 891-2380: A cocktail bar and restaurant designed as an ode to the historic speakeasies that once inhabited Printer's Alley. Black Rabbit's building dates back to the 1890s and once served as the law office of Frank Ragano, legal counsel to Jimmy Hoffa. **New American Restaurant - Menu:** www.blackrabbittn.com/

menu

Daddy's Dogs - 201 Printers Alley: A beloved local establishment, Daddy's Dogs made its Nashville debut from a street cart in 2015, later growing to include five additional venues and three street carts. Their Printer's Alley location, a recent addition in 2021, is a **walk-up window** that perfectly complements the Alley's vibe with its **gourmet hot dog offerings**. Menu: www.daddysdogs.com/menu

Fleet Street Pub - 207 Printers Alley #101 - (615) 200 0782: Fleet Street Pub stands out as the ultimate destination for watching international soccer matches in Nashville. This English-style pub creates an authentic atmosphere with traditional English cuisine in a cozy downstairs setting reminiscent of a basement. **English Pub - Menu:** www.fleetstreetpub.com/#section-menu

Gray and Dudley - 222 3rd Ave N - (615) 610-6460: Honoring the historical legacy of the former Gray & Dudley Hardware Company, this family-owned and operated establishment proudly presents a menu with Southern delicacies and hosts an exceptional **weekend brunch** experience. **American Restaurant - Menu:** www.grayanddudley.com/menus

Sinatra Bar & Lounge - 222 4th Ave N - (615) 866-2224: A tribute to Frank Sinatra's life and legacy, this elegant restaurant has a rat-pack era style with live music daily, Italian cooking, and craft cocktails. Private dining is available. **Brunch** on Sundays. **Italian Restaurant - Menu:** www.sinatranashville.com/menu

Skull's Rainbow Room - 222 Printers Alley - (615) 810-9631: A speakeasy-style lounge that initially opened in 1948, Skull's Rainbow

Room is one of the most celebrated and revered dining experiences in Music City. Savor the delicious southern & cajun-style menu while enjoying live jazz bands featured nightly at Nashville's only downtown jazz lounge. Additionally, experience the nationally recognized late-night **burlesque show** that takes center stage on weekends. **French American Coastal Cuisine - Menu:** www.skullsrainbowroom.com/menu.

Music Venues & Bars in Printer's Alley:

Bourbon Street Blues and Boogie Bar - 220 Printers Alley: A blues and Mardi Gras-themed music club in Printer's Alley that features live music seven nights a week. www.bourbonstreetbluesandboogiebar.com/

Dirty Little Secret - 210 Printers Alley: A vibrant component of Dream Hotels, brings the essence of a Las Vegas-style nightclub to life. With DJ performances and an inviting dance floor every Friday and Saturday night. Stay tuned to Dirty Little Secret's event calendar as they frequently roll out the red carpet for celebrity guest entertainers. https://nashvilledowntown.com/go/dirty-little-secret

Lonnie's Western Room - 308 Church Street: Open since 1989, Lonnie's is a dive bar and one of Nashville's best spots for karaoke. https://lonnieswesternroom.com/

Rare Bird—200 4th Ave North, Top Floor: This rooftop bar at the boutique hotel Noelle offers an enchanting experience. It is a coveted spot to savor the essence of Nashville's nightlife, with panoramic views of the iconic Batman building and the serene Cumberland River. www.rarebirdrooftop.com/nashville

Skull's Rainbow Room - 222 Printers Alley: This is a restaurant and a jazz and blues club. www.skullsrainbowroom.com/

* * *

Fifth + Broadway - Mixed Use Assembly Hall

Located across from Bridgestone Arena, **Fifth + Broadway** houses one of the **largest food halls in the United States**, spanning over 100,000 square feet. It houses more than 30 eateries and bars, offering visitors a wide variety of culinary options, including iconic Nashville dishes like Prince's Hot Chicken, The Pharmacy Burger, Chilangos Tacos, and DeSano Pizzeria. **Address - 5036 Broadway**

This vibrant location offers visitors an **immersive shopping experience**, surrounded by **diverse retail shopping and dining options**. Fifth + Broadway is a great place to explore.

Fine Dining & Live Music inside Fifth + Broadway:

- Eddie V's Prime Seafood
- Honky Tonk
- Skydeck: **Nashville's largest rooftop patio and concert venue.**
- The Rooftop Bar
- The Supper Club
- The Twelve Thirty Club

Go to www.fifthandb.com/stores for more information and a complete list of restaurants and retail stores.

5

EAST NASHVILLE

East Nashville is known for: Hip Bars & Restaurants

Located on the east side of the Cumberland River, East Nashville, popularly known as "East Nasty," is known for its vibrant scene and hip bars & restaurants. The neighborhood's historic architecture, tree-lined streets, and charming homes contribute to its distinctive character.

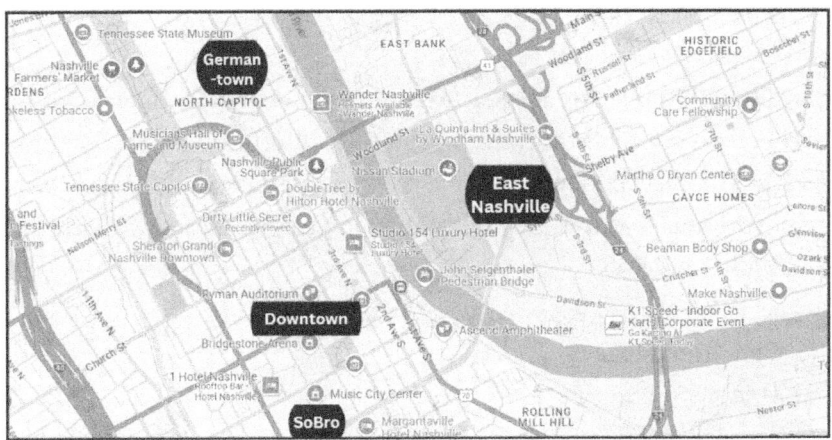

@2025 Google, Nashville Davidson County - (Downtown · Nashville, TN, USA, n.d.)

Hotels

The Dive Motel & Swim Club - 1414 Dickerson Pike - (615) 931-7114: A retro-themed motel that features a pool, hot tub, and sauna open to guests. The on-site bar and lounge are also open to the public, making it a vibrant social hub. www.thedivemotel.com

- Pets: Allowed with a one-time $50 fee
- Price: $$

The Gallatin Hotel Nashville - 2510 Gallatin Ave - (615) 861-1634: This unique hotel offers a variety of rooms and suites for guests to choose from, providing a comfortable and stylish lodging experience. www.thegallatinhotel.com

- Pets: Not allowed

- Price: $$-$$$

The Russell Hotel - 819 Russell Street - (615) 861-9535: Housed within a 115-year-old historic church, The Russell offers a one-of-a-kind boutique hotel experience. The Russell boasts 23 distinctive rooms with many original features, including stained glass windows. www.russellnashville.com

- Pets: Not allowed
- Price: $$-$$$

Urban Cowboy Bed & Breakfast - 1603 Woodland Street - (347) 840-0525: A trendy bed and breakfast known for its hip and artistic decor, this boutique hotel has a unique and charming atmosphere. Located approximately 10 minutes away from Nissan Stadium. www.urbancowboy.com/nashville/

- Pets: Allowed by request only and with a $50/day pet fee.
- Price: $$-$$$

Waymore's Guest House & Casual Club - 811 Main Street - (615) 650-9075: A boutique hotel with 93 guest rooms, suites, and bunkrooms, it offers a variety of accommodations to suit different preferences. This establishment is known for its low-key and locally-beloved atmosphere. www.waymoresnashville.com

- Pets: Allowed with an additional fee
- Price: $$-$$$

* * *

Music Venues

NOTE: Some venues require advance ticket purchases. Review venue calendars before your visit to purchase tickets in advance for desired shows or concerts.

Basement East - 917 Woodland Ave: A renowned music venue known for hosting a diverse range of live music events and shows. www.thebasementnashville.com

East Side Bowl - 1508A Gallatin Pike South: Live music venue with bowling, arcade games, a diner, and a lounge. Known for its 16-lane bowling alley, this venue goes beyond traditional bowling; it offers a unique hyper-bowling concept. www.eastsidebowl.com

The East Room - 2412 Gallatin Ave: Music and Comedy. Known for hosting live music performances, stand-up comedy shows, and various entertainment events. www.theeastroomnashville.com

The 5 Spot - 1006 Forest Ave: The 5 Spot is primarily a live music venue known for its lively atmosphere, where you can enjoy various genres of music. https://the5spot.club/

The Bowery Vault - 2905C Gallatin Pike 2nd Level Suite C: A multi-purpose venue, The Bowery Vault offers a combination of shopping, espresso bar, drinks, and live music in an intimate setting. www.theboweryvault.com

* * *

Restaurants

Fine Dining

Butcher & Bee - 902 Main St - (615) 229-5019: A hip location offering a rotating menu of creative seasonal cuisine made with local ingredients. Butcher & Bee is known for its emphasis on craft foods, including dishes made from heirloom vegetables and pasture-raised meats. **American Restaurant - Menu:** www.butcherandbee.com/nashville

Graze - 1888 Eastland Ave - (615) 686-1060: A vegan bistro & bar offering plant-based breakfast, lunch & dinner options, and a smoothie juice bar. They have Brunch daily at 3 pm. **Vegan Restaurant - Menu:** www.grazenashville.com

Inside Folk - 823 Meridian St - (615) 610-2595: A casual neighborhood restaurant guided by acclaimed chef and Rolf & Daughters' visionary Philip Krajeck, their seasonal menu uses produce from our local farmer friends. Accepts groups of 8-20 people and offers family-style dining with a menu that is prepared weekly, ensuring freshness and variety. **American Restaurant - Menu:** www.goodasfolk.com

Lockeland Table - 1520 Woodland St - (615) 228-4864: A rustic, rehabbed storefront serving classic Southern dishes and wood-fired pizzas. This community kitchen and bar offers both outdoor and indoor seating for diners. Reservations are strongly encouraged. **American Restaurant - Menu:** www.lockelandtable.com/menu

Margot Cafe & Bar - 1017 Woodland St - (615) 227-4668: A popular dining establishment known for its rotating, rustic French and Italian cuisine. This restaurant has a cozy and inviting atmosphere. **French**

EAST NASHVILLE

Restaurant - Menu: www.margotcafe.com

Peninsula - 1035 W Eastland Ave - (615) 679-0377: Modern Spanish & French cooking, plus a deep wine list, served in old-world, intimate surroundings. **Spanish & French - Menu:** www.peninsulanashville.com

The Treehouse - 1011 Clearview Ave - (615) 454-4201: A farm-to-table dining experience, this restaurant is housed in a former family home and features handcrafted wooden tables and a patio area. It is known for its locally sourced ingredients and chef-driven menu, which includes vegetarian and vegan options and carefully crafted cocktails. **American Restaurant - Menu:** www.treehousenashville.com

Two Ten Jack - 1900 Eastland Ave - (615) 454-9255: This chic and modern restaurant offers Japanese small plates, ramen and sushi, craft cocktails, and a patio. **Izakaya Restaurant - Menu:** www.twotenjack.com/nashville/

Casual Dining

- **Boston Commons** - 1008 Woodland St: New England-style seafood and fried chicken
- **Edley's BBQ** - 1004 Woodland St: BBQ: fried chicken and catfish
- **El Fuego Mexican** - 3917 Gallatin Pike: Mexican & Latin American
- **Five Points Pizza** - 1012 Woodland St: New York Style Pizza
- **JoyLand** - 901 Woodland Street: Great burgers & fried chicken
- **Mas Tacos** - 732 Mcferrin Ave: Casual Mexican food
- **Mitchell Delicatessen** - 1306 McGavock Pk: Deli Style Menu
- **Pharmacy Burger Parlour & Beer Garden** - 731 Mcferrin Ave: Burgers, brats, beer, milkshakes

- **Red Headed Stranger** - 305 Arrington St: Casual Tex-Mex
- **Rosepepper Cantina** - 1907 Eastland Ave: Nashville's best margarita & the famous sign - Mexican food
- **The Grilled Cheeserie** - 2003 Belcourt Ave: Sandwiches & milkshakes
- **TKO** - 4204 Gallatin Pike: Chinese food with a southern twist - Great for take-out

Bars

- **5 Spot** - 1006 Forest Ave: Live Music venue and bar
- **Attaboy** - 8 Mcferrin Ave: Cocktail Bar
- **Beyond the Edge Sports Bar** - 112 S 11th St
- **Boombozz Craft Pizza & Taphouse** - 1003 Russell St: Has a huge playground
- **Chopper** - 1100B Stratton Avenue: VOTED NASHVILLE SCENE'S BEST BAR 2022! Tiki Bar theme. (*CHOPPER*, n.d.)
- **Dino's Dive Bar** - 411 Gallatin Ave: East Nashville's oldest dive bar
- **East Side Bowl** - 1508A Gallatin Pike S: New Bowling Alley, Arcade, Restaurant, and live music venue
- **Inglewood Lounge** - 3914 Gallatin Pike: Bar & Pub with great Cocktails
- **Lipstick Lounge** - 1400 Woodland Stree: A gay-friendly and welcoming bar for all humans. They have trivia, bingo, cigars, and karaoke.
- **Mickeys Tavern** - 2907 Gallatin Pike - Neighborhood bar and pub
- **Noble's Kitchen & Beer Hall** - 974 Main St
- **Pearl Diver** - 1008 Gallatin Ave: Cuban fare in an island-themed bar
- **Rosemary & Beauty Queen** - 1102 Forest Ave: Burritos, sandwiches, and wraps

- **Tailgate Brewery** - 811 Gallatin Ave: Craft Brewery & Pizza with dog-friendly patio.
- **TreeHouse** - 1011 Clearview Ave: Restaurant and bar
- **Up-Down Arcade Bar** - 927 Woodland St: They have over 80 games that cost 25 cents each. Beer & Pizza
- **Urban Cowboy Public House** - 1603 Woodland St: A trendy bar inside the Urban Cowboy East Nashville Hotel.
- **Village Pub & Beer Garden** - 1308 McGavock Pk: Unpretentious neighborhood watering hole with draft beer & a pool table.
- **Vinyl Tap** - 1004 Woodland St: Record Store & Bar Combo - very local!

Desserts

- **Babycakes Bakery:** 819 Main St #1
- **Brightside Bakeshop - East:** 713 Porter Road
- **Donut Distillery:** 311 Gallatin Ave
- **East Park Donuts:** 700 Main St
- **Five Daughters Bakery - East Nashville:** 1900 Eastland Ave #101
- **HiFi Cookies:** 733 Porter Road
- **Jeni's Splendid Ice Creams:** 1892 Eastland Ave
- **Tabla Rasa Cafe:** 2039 Greenwood Ave

Coffee

- **Barista Parlor:** 519 Gallatin Ave B
- **Bongo Java East:** 107 S 11th St ·
- **East Park Donuts & Coffee:** 700 Main Street
- **Elegy Coffee:** 2909a gallatin pike
- **Frothy Monkey:** 1701 Fatherland St
- **Hanna Bee Coffee:** 1035 W Eastland Ave #1045

- **International Tea & Coffee Company:** 1100 Fatherland St, STE 104
- **Portland Brew:** 1921 Eastland Ave
- **Retrograde Coffee:** 1305 Dickerson Pike
- **Sip Cafe:** 3939 Gallatin Pike
- **Slow Hand Coffee & Bakeshop:** 1012 Gallatin Ave
- **Ugly Mugs Coffee & Tea:** 1886 Eastland Ave

6

GERMANTOWN

Germantown is known for: Restaurants and The Sounds Baseball Games.

Germantown is one of Nashville's oldest neighborhoods. It is located north of downtown and spans 18 city blocks. Named after the European immigrants who settled here in the mid-19th century, Germantown has a rich cultural and architectural heritage. Over the years, it has become one of Nashville's hottest urban neighborhoods.

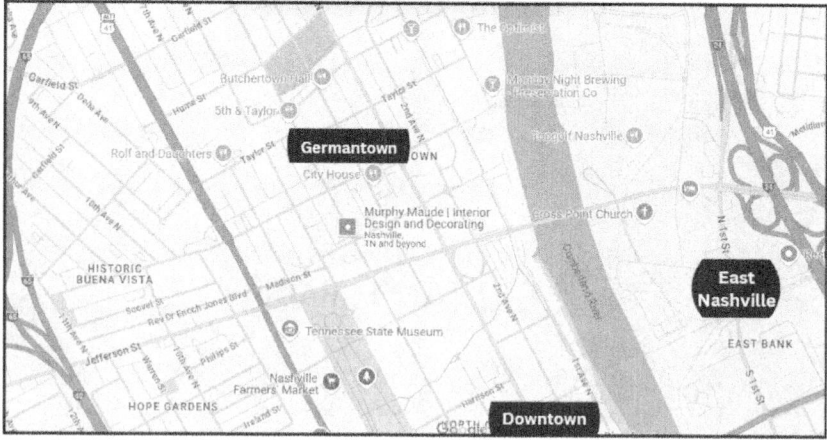

@2025 Google, Nashville Davidson County - (Downtown · Nashville, TN, USA, n.d.)

Hotels

The Germantown Inn - 1218 6th Ave N - (615) 581-1218: This charming and luxurious boutique hotel offers an exceptional stay experience, combining modern luxury with the neighborhood's rich heritage. www.germantowninn.com

- Pets: Allowed for a one-time $50 fee
- Price: $$-$$$

* * *

Music Venues

Brooklyn Bowl - 925 3rd Ave N: A music venue and bowling alley with 19 bowling lanes, a bar featuring locally crafted beers, food by the acclaimed Blue Ribbon restaurant group, and a patio overlooking First Horizon Park where the Sounds play. The venue has been voted Pollstar 2022's Best New Concert Venue (*Bowl, B.* 2023) www.brooklynbowl.com/nashville

* * *

Restaurants

Fine Dining

5th & Taylor - 1411 5th Ave N - (615) 242-4747: 5th & Taylor is Chef Daniel Lindley's homage to the American family meal. Refined American fare is served in lofty, rustic-industrial surroundings with a tree-lined patio. **New American Restaurant - Menu:** www.5thandtaylor.com

City House - 1222 4th Ave N - (615) 736-5838: Led by James Beard Award-winning Chef Tandy Wilson. A popular Italian spot serves pizza, pasta & housemade sausage. The restaurant also offers private dining options. **Italian Restaurant - Menu:** www.cityhousenashville.com

Henrietta Red - 1200 4th Ave N - (615) 490-8042: An airy, chic Oyster Bar Restaurant with elevated seafood, small plates, plus a separate bar for cocktails. **Oyster Bar & Seafood Restaurant - Menu:** www.henriettared.com

Monell's Dining - 1235 6th Ave N - (615) 248-4747: All-you-can-eat Southern fare, including fried chicken, catfish, cornbread, collard greens, and more, all served in generous portions, served family-style in historic surroundings. **Southern Restaurant - Menu:** www.monellstn.com

Rolf & Daughters - 700 Taylor St - (615) 866-9897: The restaurant's chef, Philip Krajeck, creates seasonal dishes. The restaurant's interior is designed to give you a reclaimed industrial look with exposed piping and red brick walls. **New American Restaurant - Menu:** www.rolfanddaughters.com

Sedona Taphouse - 1120 3rd Ave N - (615) 933-4260: Enjoy hundreds of craft beers, cocktails, steaks, seafood, and a great Happy Hour. **New American Restaurant - Menu:** www.sedonataphouse.com/locations/nashville-tn

The Optimist - 1400 Adams St - (615) 709-3156: Cool, brick-lined eatery for oysters, meat plates, seafood, cocktails & an impressive wine list. **Seafood Restaurant - Menu:** www.theoptimistrestaurant.com

Casual Dining

- **312 Pizza Company -** 371 Monroe Street
- **Big Al's Deli -** 1828 4th Ave North
- **Butchertown Hall -** 1416 4th Ave North: American & Tex-Mex, brews & cocktails
- **Emmy Squared Pizza -** 1121 5th Ave North
- **Farmer's Market -** 900 Rosa L Parks Blvd: This year-round market has a food court with artisanal food, restaurants, shops, and crafts. Great for shopping and lunch.

- **Germantown Cafe** – 1200 5th Ave North: Deli restaurant
- **Germantown Pub** – 708 Monroe Street: Bar & Pub
- **Jack Brown's Beer & Burger Joint** – 1123 3rd Ave North
- **Jonathans Grille– Downtown** – 717 3rd Ave North: Sports bar & restaurant
- **Mother's Ruin** – 1239 6th Ave North: Cocktail bar with shareable plates and burgers
- **The Goat – Germantown** – 1220 2nd Ave North, #100
- **Waldo's Chicken & Beer** – 1120 4th Ave North

Bars

- **Butchertown Hall** – 1416 4th Ave North: Bar & Pub
- **Frankie J's** – 1314 6th Ave North: LGBTQ+ Bar & Pub
- **Green Hour Cocktail & Absinthe Lounge** – 1201 5th Ave North: Cocktail Bar
- **Jonathans Grille – Downtown** – 717 3rd Ave North: Great sports bar & restaurant
- **Mother's Ruin** – 1239 6th Ave North: Cocktail bar with shareable plates and burgers
- **Neighbors of Germantown** – 313 Jefferson Street: Great sports bar
- **The Back Corner** – 1411 5th Ave North: Nightclub with eclectic DJs and bar
- **The Germantown Pub** – 708 Monroe Street: Bar & Pub
- **Von Elrods Beer Hall & Kitchen** – 1004 4th Ave North: Combines the beer hall concept with an in-house butchery, bakery, wood grill, and smoker.

Desserts

- **NoBaked Cookie Dough:** 1120 4th Ave North, Suite #102
- **Rolled 4 Ever Ice Cream:** 1120 4th Ave North, Suite #102
- **Tempered Fine Chocolates:** 1201 5th Ave North, Suite #103
- **The Cupcake Collection:** 1213 6th Ave North

Coffee

- **Barista Parlour:** 1230 4th Ave North
- **Elegy Coffee – Germantown:** 1390 Adams Street, Suite 13
- **Farm City Coffee:** 900 Rosa L Parks Blvd
- **Moonshot Coffee Bar:** 300 Gay Street
- **Red Bicycle Coffee & Crepes:** 1200 5th Ave North, Suite #104
- **Surefire Coffee Co:** 1421b 2nd Ave North
- **Steadfast Coffee:** 603 Taylor Street
- **Steamboys:** 1200 2nd Ave North
- **Taylor Street Coffee & Tea:** 100 Taylor Street, Suite A-23
- **Yin Yang Tea:** 83 Van Buren Street

7

THE GULCH

The Gulch is known for: Hip and Trendy Restaurants, Boutiques, and Hotels

A vibrant and dynamic neighborhood situated between Nashville's iconic Music Row and Downtown, The Gulch offers walkability and a lively atmosphere. Visitors can explore a wide range of experiences in this neighborhood, from trendy boutiques and art galleries to delicious dining options.

The Gulch is the first LEED ND (Neighborhood Development) neighborhood in the South, emphasizing sustainability and eco-friendliness (*The Gulch, 2023*).

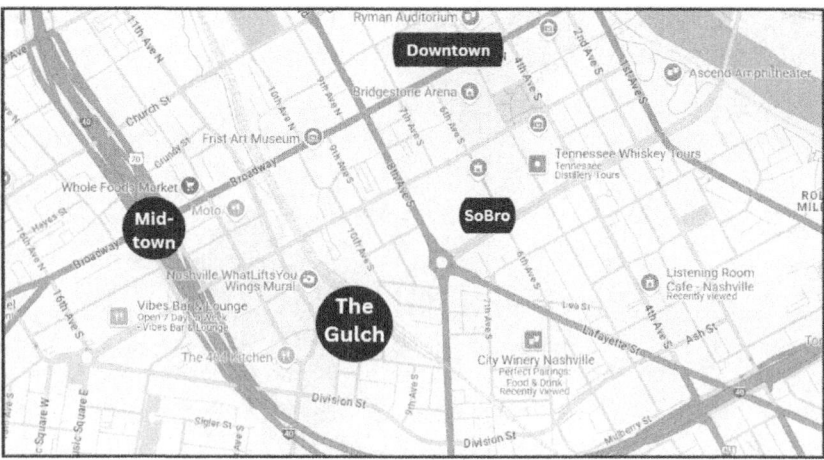

@2025 Google, Nashville Davidson County - (Downtown · Nashville, TN, USA, n.d.)

Hotels

JW Marriott - 201 8th Ave South - (615) 291-8600: Just steps from Broadway and adjacent to the Music City Center, you can revel in panoramic views of the city skyline from every room. A rooftop pool deck is surrounded by chic cabanas, an elegant pool bar and grill, and cocktail lounges throughout the property. www.marriott.com

- Pets: Allowed with a $100/night pet fee
- Price: $$$-$$$$$

The 404 Hotel - 404 12th Ave S A - (615) 242-7404: With just four suites, this boutique luxury hotel offers an intimate and exclusive experience. All suites are spacious king suites featuring separate sitting areas for added comfort **and can sleep up to 12.** The 404 Hotel takes pride in its "invisible service," ensuring guests enjoy personalized and discreet attention during their stay. Additionally, free parking is included. www.the404hotel.com

- Pets: Not allowed
- Price: Call for a price

The Westin Nashville - 807 Clark Place - 844-208-2586: This hotel features a rooftop lounge and pool. With its prime location near iconic Nashville attractions and with a range of amenities, The Westin in The Gulch is an appealing choice for travelers seeking a comfortable and centrally located accommodation option in Nashville. www.marriott.com

- Pets: Allowed with a fee of $50/night or $150/max
- Price: $$$$-$$$$$

Thompson Nashville Hotel - The Hyatt - 401 11th Ave S - (615) 262-6000: A luxury hotel offering a sophisticated urban retreat. The hotel boasts guest rooms with floor-to-ceiling windows that provide stunning views of The Gulch and downtown Nashville—just steps from art, culture, and music. www.hyatt.com

- Pets: Allowed with no additional fee
- Price: $$$$-$$$$$

W Nashville Hotel - 300 12th Ave S - (615) 379-9000: With its aesthetic designed by the renowned Rockwell Group, this hotel features rooms with a hint of retro jet-age charm, combining sleek lines and modern design. One of the standout features of the W Nashville is its impressive **10,000-square-foot hotel pool deck, the largest of its kind in Nashville.** *(W Nashville, 2023)* www.Marriott.com

- Pets: Allowed with a one-time $100 fee
- Price: $$$$-$$$$$

* * *

Music Venues

NOTE: Some shows require advance ticket purchases. Review the event schedule before your visit to secure tickets for desired shows or concerts.

Cannery Hall - 1 Cannery Row: This historic venue is Nashville's largest independently owned music venue *(Cannery Hall, 2023)*. With a deep connection to the local music scene, The Cannery is known for hosting various musical events, from intimate concerts to performances by established and emerging artists. **For tickets:** https://canneryhall.com/

Rudy's Jazz Room - 809 Gleaves Street: Rudy's is the city's premier jazz club and offers an exceptional live music experience. This intimate venue provides a cozy and casual atmosphere for jazz enthusiasts to enjoy world-class performances. Guests can savor the flavors of New Orleans cuisine while listening to jazz melodies. **For tickets:** www.rudysjazzroom.com

Sambuca - 601 12th Ave South: Live music and dancing nightly. Various musical genres, including jazz, classic rock, pop, and top 40 hits, complement a diverse dining menu. www.sambucanashville.com/live-music

The Green Light Bar - 833 Hawkins Street: Live music and sports bar.

A newcomer to the city's bar scene, this trendy establishment is known for its live music, patio, innovative cocktails, and lively atmosphere. https://thegreenlightbar.com/

The Station Inn - 402 12th Ave South: This iconic establishment has been a staple in Nashville's music scene for over 40 years. It is recognized for its commitment to preserving the classic Nashville music tradition. It has earned a reputation as a premiere listening room for bluegrass and roots music. Seats are first-come, first-served. **For tickets**: http://stationinn.com/

* * *

Restaurants

Fine Dining

Adele's - 1210 McGavock St - (615) 988-9700: Enjoy elevated farm-to-fork comfort food housed in a repurposed auto repair garage. The restaurant features an open kitchen with a large fireplace grill and wood-burning oven, offering a menu that emphasizes fresh, seasonal ingredients sourced from local farms. It also offers a popular weekend brunch buffet and a selection of bespoke cocktails, hard-to-find whiskeys, and wines. **New American Restaurant - Menu:** www.adelesrestaurant.com/location/adeles-nashville/

Bourbon Steak by Michael Mina - 201 8th Ave S - (629) 208-8440: *Reservations are required, and **there is a dress code**, so call ahead.* Swanky restaurant led by Michelin Star chef Michael Mina on the 34th floor of the JW Marriott with 360-degree views of downtown. **Steaks and**

Seafood Restaurant - Menu: https://nashvillebourbonsteak.com/

Carne Mare - 300 12th Ave S - (615) 379-9000: An Italian chophouse offering a menu curated by James Beard Award-Winning Chef Andrew Carmellini (Corbin, 2021). Specializing in prime cuts of steaks, fine seafood, and Italian specialties. **Italian Restaurant - Menu:** www.carnemarenashville.com

Chauhan Ale and Masala House - 123 12th Ave N - (615) 242-8426: This restaurant is known for its innovative fusion of Indian and American flavors. Co-owned by Executive Chef Maneet Chauhan, a prominent figure in the culinary world, the restaurant offers a unique dining experience. **Indian Restaurant - Menu:** www.chauhannashville.com

Kayne Prime - 1103 McGavock St - (615) 259-0050: A renowned upscale steakhouse, this chef-chic boutique restaurant boasts an extensive menu featuring premium cuts of steak and various other delectable dishes. Known for its sophisticated ambiance and impeccable service. **Steakhouse - Menu:** www.mstreetnashville.com/kayne-prime

Marsh House - 401 11th Ave S - (615) 262-6001: Known for its commitment to serving responsibly sourced and sustainable seafood with a seasonal menu. Marsh House has become a popular destination for those seeking a seafood-centric and eco-conscious dining experience in the city. **Seafood Restaurant - Menu:** www.marshhouserestaurant.com

Moto Cucina + Enoteca - 1120 McGavock St - (615) 736-5305: This restaurant offers a contemporary Italian dining experience, blending rustic-modern cuisine with a chic, industrial ambiance. The menu emphasizes seasonal, locally sourced ingredients, featuring house-made pasta and a variety of small plates. Complementing the culinary offerings is an extensive, award-winning wine list, focusing on selections available by the glass "enoteca style." (*About - Moto Cucina + Enoteca*, n.d.) **Italian Restuarant - Menu:** www.mstreetnashville.com/moto

Saint Añejo - 1120 McGavock St - (615) 736-5301: This restaurant offers a dynamic dining experience focusing on Mexican cuisine and craft cocktails. Saint Anejo's menu features a wide range of delicious Mexican dishes, from tacos and enchiladas to fresh guacamole and flavorful salsas, and more than 100 tequilas to pick from. **Mexican Restaurant - Menu:** www.mstreetnashville.com/saint-anejo

Sambuca - 601 12th Ave S - (615) 248-2888: A hip spot for dinner, live music and dancing. Known as Nashville's only rockin' restaurant, Sambuca offers a diverse American menu complemented by nightly live music, creating a lively dining experience. The restaurant also features a rooftop patio with views of the Nashville skyline, making it a popular spot for dining and entertainment. **New American Restaurant - Menu:** www.sambucarestaurant.com

The 404 Kitchen - 507 12th Ave S - (615) 251-1404: Farm-to-table New American fare and craft cocktails are served in chic digs, plus a basement bar. This renowned restaurant is led by Chef Matt Bolus and is known for offering a modern twist on classic European cuisine. The 404 Kitchen also features Gertie's Whiskey Bar, which boasts one of the South's most extensive whiskey selections. **New American Restaurant - Menu:** www.the404nashville.com

Virago - 507 12th Ave S - (615) 251-1404: This pioneering restaurant is known for its elevated dining experience and progressive Asian cuisine.

Virago's is a hip hangout for Japanese cuisine, sushi, and cocktails. It has a sophisticated, modern ambiance, with secluded booths and private dining rooms. **Hip Sushi & Japanese Cuisine - Menu:** www.the404nashville.com

Casual Dining

- **Arnolds Country Kitchen** - 605 8th Ave South: Family-owned "meat and three" served from a cafeteria-style steam table.
- **Bar Louie - Gulch** - 314 11th Ave South: American grub & happy-hour deals.
- **Biscuit Love** - 316 11th Ave South: Breakfast, Brunch, & Lunch.
- **Burger Republic** - 420 11th Ave South
- **Emmy-Squared Pizza** - 404 12th Ave South
- **Milk & Honey** - 214 11th Ave South: Brunch restaurant, juice bar, baked goods, sandwiches.
- **Party Fowl** - 719 8th Ave South: Fried Chicken & the biggest Bloody Mary you have ever seen and also known for its Brunch.
- **Peg Leg Porker** - 903 Gleaves St: Soulful BBQ. Good for watching sports.
- **Snooze, an A.M. Eatery** - 801 Division St: Breakfast & Brunch restaurant.
- **St.Vito Focacceria** - 605 Mansion St: Pizza and Italian, great for take-out.
- **The Gumbo Brothers** - 505 12th Ave South: Cajun, great for happy hour and watching sports.
- **Two Hands** - 606 8th Ave South: Casual Australian-inspired cafe & bar.

Bars

- **16-Bit Bar+Arcade** - 1102 Grundy St: (It will say Pins Mechanical Co. on the building.) A retro-themed bar with classic arcade games, old-school cocktails, and craft brews. It also features duckpin bowling, 40+ pinball machines, old-school entertainment, an outdoor patio with beer pong, and more.
- **Bar Louie - Gulch** - 314 11th Ave South: Known for cocktails, craft beers, and shareable plates.
- **Cumberland Bar** - 201 8th Ave South: Elegant lobby bar inside JW Marriott.
- **Gertie's Whiskey Bar** - 507 12th Ave South: Upscale whiskey-focused bar with a diverse selection of bourbons and cocktails. In the basement of The 404 Kitchen.
- **Golden Sound Nashville** - 610 Magazine St: Cocktail bar in historic location.
- **Hops & Crafts Taproom** - 319 12th Ave South: Extensive local and regional craft beer selection, with light pub fare.
- **Neighbors Gulch** - 610 12th Ave S: Casual restaurant and bar known for cocktails, happy hour, and small plates.
- **Sedona Taphouse** - 809 Ewing Ave: A restaurant and craft beer bar known for its extensive selection of local and international beers on tap, handcrafted cocktails, and a scratch-made menu.
- **The Green Light Bar** - 833 Hawkins Street: In the Edgehill/Gulch area, this British Pub has sports and a vibrant atmosphere. Check their calendar of events for poker night, trivia, karaoke, themed parties, open mic comedy, and live music! For event calendar: www.thegreenlightbar.com
- **The Pub Nashville** - 400 11th Ave South: Cozy British pub with a wide selection of beers, ales, and pub food.

Rooftop Bars

- **L27 Rooftop Lounge** – 807 Clark Place: A multi-level bar on the 27th floor of The Westin Hotel. Hosts various winter pop-ups.
- **L.A. Jackson** – 401 11th Ave South: This swanky bar is located on the top floor of the Thompson Nashville Hotel.
- **Proof** – 300 12th Ave S: An indoor/outdoor rooftop bar inside the W Nashville Hotel.
- **Up Rooftop Table & Tavern** – 901 Division St: Rooftop bar and restaurant inside Fairfield Inn & Suites. Known for being the first indoor/outdoor rooftop bar in Nashville. (*UP Rooftop Table and Tavern | Official Site*, n.d.)

Desserts

- **The Nashville Sundae Club:** 335 11th Ave South
- **Five Daughters Bakery:** 602 12th Ave South – located inside The Icon.
- **Tiff's Treats Cookie Delivery:** 137 12th Ave N – great for pre-order or delivery. Limited selection for walk-ins.

Coffee

- **Barista Parlour:** 300 12th Ave South – located inside W Nashville.
- **Honest Coffee Roasters:** 803 Lea Ave – located inside 805 Lea.
- **Killebrew Coffee:** 401 11th Ave South – located inside Thompson Nashville.
- **Stompin' Grounds Market:** 201 8th Ave South – located inside JW Marriott.
- **Tin Cup Coffee:** 1201 Demonbreun St – located inside Capstar Tower.

8

MIDTOWN, MUSIC ROW, & WEST END

Midtown is known for: Partying, Hotels, & Restaurants.

Midtown is situated between downtown Nashville, Music Row, and West End. Midtown boasts a vibrant nightlife with numerous bars, restaurants, and live music venues.

* * *

Music Row is known for: Record Labels, Studios, Publishing Companies, and all things Music Industry.

Music Row is a renowned and iconic district that plays a pivotal role in the Country Music industry. This historic area, located southwest of downtown Nashville, is often called the heart of the country music business.

While Music Row isn't known for bars and restaurants like Lower Broadway, it features statues and monuments that pay homage to country music legends and stately old homes repurposed into recording studios, publishing houses, and record label offices. Drive through the area to see where aspiring musicians have made their mark in the music industry.

* * *

West End is known for: The Parthenon, Centennial Park, and Vanderbilt University.

The West End neighborhood is a hub of activity and offers urban amenities and green spaces. Its historic homes, tree-lined streets, sidewalks, and front porches contribute to its charming atmosphere. West End is also home to various dining and entertainment options.

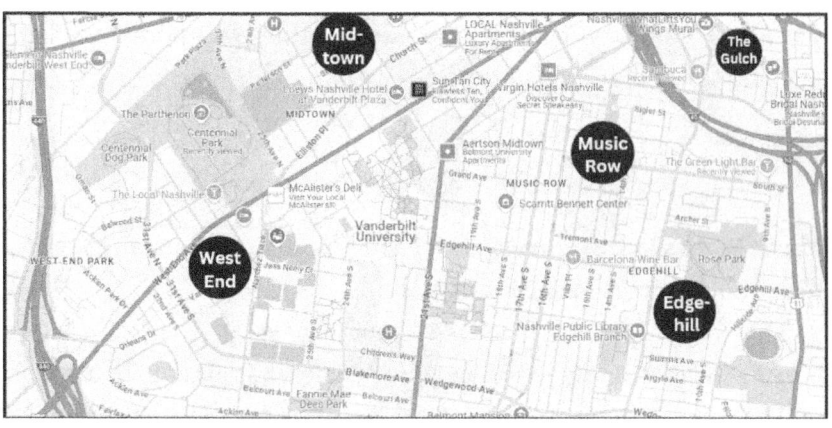

@2025 Google, Nashville Davidson County – (Downtown · Nashville, TN, USA, n.d.)

Hotels

Aloft Nashville - 1719 West End Ave - (615) 329-4200: This modern and design-inspired hotel is near Music Row and Vanderbilt University **in the West End district.** This tech-forward hotel offers a unique and lively experience. www.marriott.com - Aloft Nashville West End

- Pets: Allowed with a fee
- Price: $$

Cambria Hotel Nashville - Midtown - 1612 Church Street - (615) 931-0777: This modern hotel offers a range of amenities with Italian-inspired guest rooms. One of the hotel's highlights is its on-site restaurant and rooftop lounge called The Rux, which serves local craft beers and curated cocktails. www.cambriamidtown.com

- Pets: Not allowed
- Price: $$

Conrad Hilton Nashville—1620 West End Ave—(615) 327-8000: This luxurious 5-star hotel **in Midtown Nashville** is less than five minutes from Music Row and Vanderbilt University. It features 17,000 square feet of meeting and event space designed with a contemporary aesthetic, including floor-to-ceiling windows and a rooftop bar. The hotel is suitable for weddings, meetings, and special events. (Geheren, 2022) www.hilton.com/en/hotels/bnaleci-conrad-nashville/

- Pets: Not allowed
- Price: $$$

Element Nashville Vanderbilt West End - 4 City Blvd - (615) 320-8400:

The hotel's location **near Vanderbilt University** and the medical center makes it an ideal choice for those visiting the university or seeking medical treatment. It's also within a short walk of Centennial Park, close to Midtown, and has a vibrant music scene. www.marriott.com/element-nashville-vanderbilt-west-end/

- Pets: Allowed with a fee
- Price: $-$$

Graduate Hotel - 101 20th Ave North - (615) 551-2700: The Graduate is a charming hotel **near Vanderbilt University.** The hotel's design is inspired by the local culture and history of Music City, with a playful and eclectic aesthetic that pays tribute to Nashville's vibrant music scene. Guests can enjoy comfortable accommodations, a rooftop bar with scenic views, and delicious dining options. www.graduatehotels.com/nashville/

- Pets: Allowed with a fee
- Price: $$-$$$$

Hotel Fraye - 1810 Broadway - (615) 321-1007: A distinctive establishment **in Midtown's heart**, close to Vanderbilt and Music Row. With a rooftop pool, it is part of the Curio Collection by Hilton, known for its unique and independent hotels. www.hilton.com/en/hotels/bnamoqq-hotel-fraye-nashville-midtown/

- Pets: Allowed with a fee
- Price: $$-$$$

Hutton Hotel - 1808 West End Ave - (615) 340-9333: This hotel offers guests a distinctive blend of modern luxury and Southern hospitality

in the West End neighborhood. Situated just steps from the iconic Music Row, the Hutton Hotel houses Analog, an intimate music venue showcasing emerging and established artists. www.huttonhotel.com

- Pets: Pet-friendly with a fee
- Price: $$-$$$

Kimpton Aertson Hotel - 2021 Broadway - (615) 340-6376: Located slightly away from the tourist-heavy areas, this ideal location provides a more relaxed atmosphere **in the Music Row district.** This luxury boutique hotel offers upscale amenities, trendsetting style, and unforgettable services. The hotel is surrounded by bars and restaurants and features a rooftop pool and bar. www.aertsonhotel.com

- Pets: Allowed with no restrictions
- Price: $$-$$$

Locale Music Row - 1221 Division Street - (512) 580-7606: A contemporary apartment-style hotel in the **Music Row neighborhood.** Key features of Locale Music Row include spacious apartments equipped with kitchens, washer/dryer units, and comfortable living rooms. This setup is ideal for travelers looking for an extended stay or those who prefer the convenience of a fully equipped apartment while exploring Nashville. www.locale.com/properties/music-row

- Pets: Not allowed
- Price: $$-$$$

Lowes Vanderbilt Hotel - 2100 West End Ave - (615) 320-1700: This stylish hotel is a AAA Four-Diamond property that seamlessly blends Southern charm with modern luxury (*Loews Nashville Hotel*

Near Vanderbilt U, n.d.). The hotel is directly **across from Vanderbilt University** and offers convenient access to Music Row and Centennial Park. The hotel is suitable for leisure and business travelers, with extensive meeting and event facilities. www.loewshotels.com/vanderbilt-hotel

- Pets: Pet-friendly with a fee
- Price: $$$-$$$$$

Moxy Nashville Vanderbilt Hotel - 1911 Belcourt Ave - (615) 385-1911: Situated **in the Hillsboro Village** neighborhood, close to Music Row, this trendy, laid-back hotel has a unique and lively atmosphere. With a hip lobby bar that includes "Plug and Meet" gathering spaces. www.marriott.com/en-us/hotels/bnaov-moxy-nashville-vanderbilt-area/overview/

- Pets: Pet-friendly with a fee
- Price: $$-$$$

Placemakr Music Row - 1600 McGavock Street - (615) 227-1600: This accommodation option provides spacious and well-equipped apartments with full kitchens, laundry facilities, and comfortable living spaces, ideal for short-term and extended stays. (There is also a location in the SoBro area of downtown Nashville.) www.placemakr.com/Nashville

- Pets: Allowed with a fee
- Price: $$

The Hayes Street Hotel & Bar - 1909 Hayes Street - (615) 320-0110: This unique and homey boutique hotel is situated **in the Midtown/West**

End district of Nashville and offers close proximity to Music Row. Special rates are available for guests and patients visiting Vanderbilt Hospital. www.hayesstreethotel.com

- Pets: Allowed with a fee
- Price: $-$$

Virgin Hotels Nashville - 1 Music Square W - (615) 667-8000: A chic and modern boutique hotel **in the heart of Music Row**, this hotel is known for its contemporary, music-themed design and comfortable accommodations. The hotel also has excellent amenities, including a rooftop pool, fitness center, pool table, and various dining options. www.virginhotels.com/nashville/

- Pets: Allowed with a fee
- Price: $$-$$$$

* * *

Music Venues

Analog at Hutton Hotel - 1808 West End Ave: Located **inside the Hutton Hotel**, this unique music venue offers a blend of social club ambiance and live entertainment, providing guests with an intimate experience. **For upcoming events and tickets:** www.analognashville.com/events/

Exit Inn - 2208 Elliston Place: A renowned music venue **near Centennial Park** and Vanderbilt University. Established in 1971, it has transformed from a modest "listening room" to a vibrant 500-

capacity rock club (Exit/In, 2023). **For upcoming events and tickets:** https://exitin.com/

Live Oak - 1522 Demonbreun Street: A vibrant music venue and sports bar. **Nestled off Music Row**, it hosts **free nightly writers' rounds**, showcasing veteran and emerging songwriters. The venue features an array of televisions, extensive bars, and a stage dedicated to live music. www.liveoaknashville.com/

Musicians Corner - 2500 West End Ave: Musicians Corner is a **popular free concert series** held at the corner of West End Avenue and 27th Avenue North **within Centennial Park.** This event occurs each Spring and Fall, offering live music performances suitable for all ages (*Musicians Corner | Nashville's Free Concert Series*, n.d.). **For more information:** www.musicianscornernashville.com/

The Local Nashville - 110 28th Ave N: In the **West End area**, The Local is a neighborhood bar and live music venue renowned for its cozy atmosphere and dedication to original, local music. https://localnash.com/

Tin Roof - 1516 Demonbreun Street: Established in 2002, **near Music Row and Midtown.** The Tin Roof has a long-standing presence in the city and has become a staple venue for enjoying live music and drinks. https://theoriginaltinroof.com/

The End - 2219 Elliston Place: A small-capacity rock 'n' roll dive bar that has been a staple of the city's music scene for over 30 years. Situated on the famed "Rock Block" **near Vanderbilt University,** this intimate venue has a capacity of approximately 200 people. Known for its grunge aesthetic, The End provides a cozy atmosphere for live music seven nights a week, featuring diverse genres from punk and metal to indie and alternative rock. **For upcoming events and tickets**: https://endnashville.com/

* * *

Restaurants

Fine Dining

Amerigo Italian Restaurant - 1920 West End Ave - (615) 320-1740: A beloved local favorite offering authentic Italian cuisine for over 25 years. Known for its hand-made plates of pasta, wood-fired pizzas, fresh seafood, and flavorful wood-fired steaks. **Italian Restaurant - Menu: www.amerigo.net**

Barcelona Wine Bar - 1200 Villa Place - (615) 327-0600: Offers a warm and inviting atmosphere inspired by Spanish culture, serving a menu focused on clean flavors and seasonal ingredients. Guests can enjoy diverse tapas paired with an extensive wine list. **Spanish Restaurant - Menu: www.barcelonawinebar.com/location/nashville/**

Blue Aster - 1620 West End Ave - (615) 327-0600: Located in the Conrad Hilton Hotel and named after the iconic native flower, the Blue Aster, this locally-inspired culinary destination offers dishes with a Nashville twist, featuring fresh, local ingredients sourced from the Tennessee. **Modern American & Seafood - Menu: www.blueasternashville.com**

Chateau West - 3408 West End Ave - (615)-432-2622: In an elegant setting reminiscent of a Bordeaux chateau. The menu features classic French dishes such as Chateaubriand, Duck Chambord, and Beef Bourguignon, with fresh baguettes made daily and served with European butter. **French Restaurant - Menu:** www.chateauwestrestaurant.com/

E3 Chophouse - 1628 21st Ave South - (615) 301-1818: An upscale steakhouse known for its selection of prime steaks, seafood, and handcrafted cocktails with a refined atmosphere perfect for fine dining. In a posh, 2-story space with **a rooftop bar. Steakhouse - Menu:** e3chophousenashville.com

The Electric Jane - 1301 Demonbreun Street - (615) 964-7175: A modern dining and live entertainment venue that blends creative culture, artistic community, and culinary excellence. Positioned between Music Row and The Gulch, this trendy cocktail bar and restaurant has vegetarian options, live music, and drag shows. **American Restaurant - Reservations are required - Menu:** https://postmates.com/store/the-electric-jane/

Flemings Steakhouse - 2525 West End - (615) 342-0131: Offers an exceptional fine dining experience, specializing in steaks, seafood, and an extensive selection of wines. Located across from Centennial Park and near Vanderbilt Stadium. **Steakhouse - Menu:** www.flemingssteakhouse.com/locations/tn/nashville

Giovanni Ristorante - 909 20th Ave S - (615) 760-5932: Established in 2008 after relocating from Midtown Manhattan, this restaurant has become a staple in Nashville's culinary scene (*Nashville's Best Italian Restaurant | Giovanni Ristorante*, n.d.). Under the guidance of Chef Giovanni Pinato, this venue is renowned for offering an authentic Italian dining experience. **Italian Restaurant - Menu:** giovanninashville.com

MIDTOWN, MUSIC ROW, & WEST END

Halls Chophouse - 1600 West End Ave, #101 - (615) 246-6000: Offers premium steaks, seafood, classic comfort food, and inventive cocktails in an upscale yet relaxed atmosphere. The open kitchen design allows guests to observe the culinary team in action, and live music performances add to the ambiance. **Steakhouse - Menu:** hallschophousenashville.com/

Jimmy Kelly's Steakhouse- 217 Louise Ave - (615) 329-4349: Established in 1934 and housed in a two-story stately Southern mansion, the restaurant's interior exudes classic charm. Many of the staff who have been with the establishment for decades contribute to the family atmosphere. The founder's commitment was straightforward: serve a great steak, pour a generous portion of whiskey, and ensure attentive service. This philosophy has been the cornerstone of the restaurant's enduring success (Jimmy Kelly's Steakhouse, n.d.). **Steakhouse - Menu:** jimmykellys.com/

Maggiano's Little Italy - 3106 West End Ave - (615) 514-0270: Offers guests a classic Italian-American dining experience inspired by traditional family recipes, with the option for family-style dining, which is ideal for groups. **Italian Restaurant - Menu:** maggianos.com/menus/3106-w.-end-avenue/

Sadie's Nashville - 1200 Villa Place - (615) 988-1200: Just steps from Music Row, Sadie's offers a hip & casual fine dining experience serving traditional Mediterranean dishes grilled over open flames. This all-day café provides a trendy atmosphere where patrons can enjoy brunch, lunch, cocktails, or dinner indoors or al fresco. **Mediterranean Restaurant - Menu:** sadiesnashville.com/menus/

Stoney River Steakhouse - 3015 West End Ave - (615) 340-9550:

An upscale dining experience. Known for its hand-cut steaks, fresh seafood, and signature salads. **Note: This location can accommodate private dining for groups ranging from 10-65 guests** (Stoney River, 2023). **Steakhouse Restaurant - Menu:** stoneyriver.com/3015-west-end-avenue/

SupperClub on Belcourt - 2000 Belcourt Ave - (615) 678-6431: This establishment is the brainchild of the Make A Play Hospitality Group, known for creating vibrant culinary experiences in Tennesse (*SCOB in Nashville*, n.d.). The design elements pay homage to the original supper clubs of the 1960s and 70s with chic and trendsetting decor. A DJ is spinning an eclectic blend of jazz and classics on the weekends. **American Steakhouse - Menu:** ilovesupperclub.com

The Catbird Seat - 1711 Division Street - (615) 810-8200: Securing a reservation at the Catbird Seat is an exceptionally challenging feat, partly due to its small seating capacity of just 22 spots or its restricted operating days (Wednesday to Saturday, exclusively for dinner only with two seatings per evening). What makes the Catbird Seat unique is its intimate and exclusive ambiance. Diners are seated around a U-shaped counter encircling an open central kitchen, creating an intimate and exclusive dining experience. **New American Restaurant - Menu:** thecatbirdseatrestaurant.com

Casual Dining

- **Americano Free Style Tapas -** 1 720 West End Ave, #100: Shared small plates in a casual setting.
- **Avo Nashville -** 4 City Blvd, #104: Vegan restaurant.
- **Bricktops -** 3000 West End Ave: Upscale chain.
- **Central Bar & Kitchen -** 2555 West End Ave: Inside the Marriott at

Vanderbilt. Comfort food and great happy hour. Good for watching sports.
- **Commodore Grille** - 2613 West End Ave: Hotel bar & grill with live music nightly. Inside Holiday Inn - Vanderbilt.
- **Elliston Place Soda Shop** - 2105 Elliston Place: A 1939 diner with retro decor and jukeboxes.
- **Fido** - 1812 21st Ave South: Cafe & Coffee House
- **Five Odd Fellows Food & Drink** - 1811 Broadway: Upscale tavern and gastropub.
- **Hattie B's Hot Chicken** - 112 19th Ave South
- **Hopsmith Nashville** - 1903 Division Street: American grub and chill hangout.
- **Jack Browns Beer & Burger** - 1201 Villa Pl, Suite 102: Dive bar with great burgers.
- **Jasper's** - 1918 West End Ave: Comfort food and weekend brunch.
- **Midtown Cafe** - 102 19th Ave South: American cuisine in a cozy, art-lined setting.
- **Music Row Bar & Grill** - 1000 17th Ave S: American restaurant with outdoor seating.
- **Nada** - 202 21st Ave South: Gourmet Mexican and cocktails.
- **Salsarita's Fresh Mexican Grill** - 2515 West End Ave: Counter-served Mexican Chain.
- **Scout's Pub** - 101 17th Ave South: Great happy hour. Good for watching sports.
- **Suzy Wong's House of Yum Drag 'N Brunch** - 1519 B Church St: Friday through Sunday only. Asian Fusion, brunch, and cocktails with a drag show. **Reservations for the drag show are suggested.** www.suzywongsnashville.com/
- **The Row Kitchen & Pub** - 110 Lyle Ave: Burgers, seafood, cocktails, drafts, happy hour, live music, and great for watching sports.
- **The Slider House** - 1907 Division Street: Sliders, craft beers, and

cocktails.
- **The Stillery** - 1921 Broadway: Burgers, brick-oven pizza, mason jar cocktails, live music.
- **Urban Cookhouse** - 1907 Broadway: Counter-served sandwiches & salads.

Bars

- **Bobby's Idle Hour Tavern** - 9 Music Square S: Old-school watering hole with open jam nights.
- **Broadway Brew Pub & Grub** - 1900 Broadway: Bar bites, TV sports, and bar games.
- **Central Bar & Kitchen** - 2555 West End Ave: Inside the Marriott at Vanderbilt.
- **Commodore Lounge** - 2613 West End Ave: Holiday Inn Hotel Bar.
- **Corner Bar at Elliston Place** - 2200 Elliston Pl: Basic bar grub, drinks, and TV sports.
- **Jack Browns Beer & Burger** - 1201 Villa Pl, Suite 102: Dive bar with great burgers.
- **Live Oak** - 1522 Demonbreun St: Live music, drinks, and bar food.
- **Losers Bar & Grill** - 1911 Division St: No-frills venue with classic bar grub, live music and drinks.
- **Old Glory Bar (Edgehill Village)** - 1200 Villa Pl, Suite 103: A hidden underground bar serves expertly crafted cocktails in a historic boiler room.
- **Play Dance Club** - 1519 Church St: Gay night club with drag shows and DJs.
- **Sandbar Nashville** - 3 City Ave: Beach-inspired atmosphere with sand volleyball courts, fresh fruit cocktails, and a relaxed, shoes-optional environment. Dog and family-friendly.
- **Springwater Supper Club & Lounge** - 115 27th Ave N: Dive Bar with

vintage decor, live music, and pool tables.
- **The End** - 2219 Elliston Pl: Long-running venue with full bar and live music.
- **The Patterson House** - 1711 Division St: Upscale cocktail bar and pub.
- **The Red Door Saloon Midtown** - 1816 Division St: Midtown bar with drinks, hot dogs, sandwiches, and outdoor seating.
- **The Row Kitchen & Pub** - 110 Lyle Ave: Burgers, seafood, cocktails, drafts, happy hour, live music, and great for watching sports.
- **Tribe** - 1515 Church St: Gay bar with a big dance floor and show-tune theme nights.

Rooftop Bars

- **Loser's Bar & Grill:** 1911 Division St
- **The Pool Club:** 1 Music Square W: Located inside Virgin Hotels.
- **The Rux:** 1612 Church St: Inside The Cambria Hotel Nashville Midtown.
- **White Limozeen:** 101 20th Ave N - All pink venue inside The Graduate Hotel.

Desserts

- **Cocorico Bakery & Cafe:** 1600 Division Street
- **Elliston Place Soda Shop:** 2105 Elliston Place
- **KOKOS Ice Cream Scoop Shop:** 3 City Ave
- **Marble Slab Creamery:** 2817 West End Ave
- **Parlor Doughnuts:** 1720 West End Ave
- **Sarabhas Creamery - Ice Cream & Coffee:** 400 21st Ave S
- **The Baked Bear:** 1809 Division St

Coffee

- **8th & Roast:** 116 20th Ave S
- **Carrie's Coffee:** 3102 West End Ave
- **Land of a Thousand Hills Coffee:** 805 12th Ave S
- **Fido:** 1812 21st Ave
- **High Point Coffee:** 1009B 17th Ave S
- **Just Love Coffee Cafe:** 1528 Demonbreun St
- **MR*T Nashville:** 19th Ave S, Suite 103
- **Paradeisos Coffee Company:** 2813 West End Ave
- **Poindexter Coffee:** 101 20th Ave N – inside the Graduate Hotel
- **Sump Coffee:** 8 City Blvd
- **The Well Coffeehouse Koinonia:** 1000 16th Ave S

Photo Credit: Jonathan Ross

9

OPRYLAND HOTEL

One of the U.S.'s largest and most iconic resorts, Gaylord Opryland offers a stunning indoor oasis just minutes from downtown Nashville. Spread across nine acres, Gaylord Opryland Resort feels like a world of its own, with lush gardens, waterfalls, and winding rivers all tucked beneath a massive glass atrium.

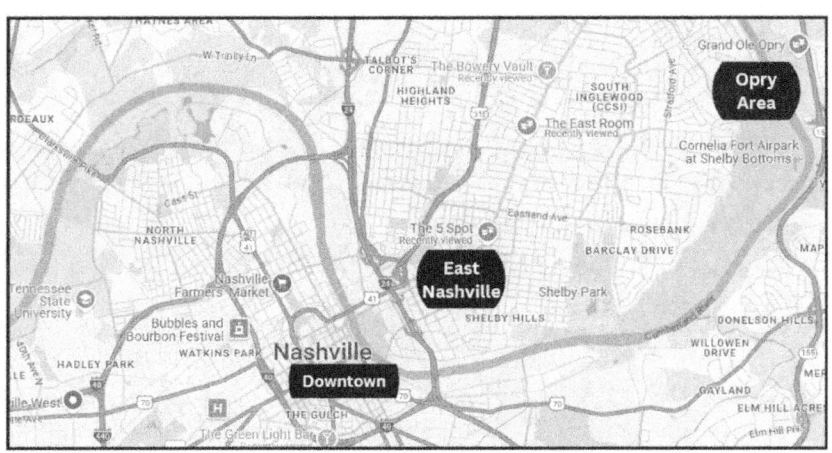

@2025 Google, Nashville Davidson County – (Downtown · Nashville, TN, USA, n.d.)

Gaylord Opryland Resort & Convention Center

- Address: 2800 Opryland Drive
- Phone: (615) 889-1000
- Link: www.marriott.com/en-us/hotels/bnago-gaylord-opryland-resort-and-convention-center
- Pets: Not allowed

No matter the weather, there's plenty to explore—from upscale dining and boutique shopping to the serene Relâche Spa. Take a relaxing boat ride along the Delta River, catch live entertainment, or walk to the legendary Grand Ole Opry. And if you visit during the holidays, the dazzling light displays and festive events make it even more magical.

Without leaving the hotel complex, you will find restaurants, shopping, desserts, coffee, and more! Opryland isn't just a hotel—it's an experience you won't forget.

General Facts:

- **Size:** Covers 9 acres of indoor gardens and waterways under a massive glass atrium.
- **Rooms:** Features over **2,800 guest rooms**, making it one of the largest hotels in the U.S.
- **Location:** Situated near the **Grand Ole Opry**, about 10 miles from downtown Nashville.

Amenities & Attractions:

- **Delta Riverboat Ride:** A quarter-mile indoor river with flatboat tours.
- **Water Park: SoundWaves:** A high-end indoor/outdoor water attraction exclusive to hotel guests.
- **Shopping & Dining:** Over **15 restaurants, bars, and cafes** offering diverse cuisine.
- **Convention Space:** More than **750,000 square feet** of event and meeting space.

Opryland Hotel Indoor Atrium – Photo Credit: Hendrickson Photography

Unique Features:

- **Indoor Gardens:** The **Conservatory, Delta,** and **Cascades** atriums house thousands of tropical plants, waterfalls, and even koi fish.

- **Holiday Lights:** One of Nashville's most famous Christmas attractions, featuring millions of twinkling lights, ice sculptures, and festive events.
- **Eco-Friendly Design:** The massive glass atrium allows for natural light and helps regulate indoor temperatures efficiently.

Whether visiting for business, a family getaway, or a romantic retreat, Opryland offers a unique experience blending luxury, nature, and entertainment (Wikipedia contributors, 2024).

Music Venues Nearby

The Grand Ole Opry - 600 Opry Mills Dr: (Go to Chapter 11 for more information on this world-famous and iconic music venue!) www.opry.com/

Music City Bar & Grill - 2416 Music Valley Dr: Late-night country music venue. This 21-and-over establishment offers live country music performances nightly.

Nashville Palace - 2611 McGavock Pk: Just steps from the Opryland Hotel's main entrance, this iconic venue offers live traditional country music, dancing, and Southern cuisine. www.thefamousnashvillepalace.com/

The Music of Nashville - 2416 Music Valley Dr: A dinner theater where guests can enjoy a buffet-style dinner and a live show featuring talented performers who pay tribute to country music legends and contemporary stars. The venue provides a family-friendly atmosphere. www.themusicofnashville.com/

III

ATTRACTIONS, CONCERT VENUES, & THE ARTS

10

LANDMARKS & MUST VISIT ATTRACTIONS

Whether you're a music fan or a history buff, you can soak up Nashville's Southern charm and vibrant music scene by checking out its iconic landmarks and attractions.

Belle Meade Historic Site & Winery - 5025 Harding Pike: Belle Meade is a beautifully preserved 19th-century plantation. Once famous for breeding thoroughbred racehorses, the estate features a grand Greek Revival mansion, historic outbuildings, and lush grounds. Visitors can explore guided tours, wine tastings at the on-site winery, and interactive exhibits highlighting the site's rich but complex history (Belle Meade Historic Site, n.d.). https://visitbellemeade.com/

Cheekwood Botanical Garden - 1200 Forrest Park Drive: Cheekwood is a stunning 55-acre estate that combines lush botanical gardens, an art museum, and historic charm. Once the home of the Cheek family, this former mansion now showcases rotating art exhibits, beautifully landscaped gardens, and seasonal events like Cheekwood in Bloom and Holiday LIGHTS (*Historic Estate in Nashville | Cheekwood Estate & Gardens*, 2025). https://cheekwood.org/

Country Music Hall of Fame - 222 Rep John Lewis Way S: Located in the SoBro area of downtown, this museum offers an immersive journey through the history of country music. It celebrates the genre's evolution and impact with extensive exhibits featuring artifacts, recordings, and memorabilia from legends like Johnny Cash, Dolly Parton, and Hank Williams. Interactive displays, rotating exhibitions, and the iconic Hall of Fame Rotunda make it a must-visit for music lovers. www.countrymusichalloffame.org/

John Seigenthaler Pedestrian Bridge - 3rd Ave S & Symphony Pl: Spanning the Cumberland River, this bridge offers some of the best panoramic views of downtown Nashville. This historic steel truss bridge, originally built in 1909, is now a pedestrian-only walkway, perfect for strolling, biking, or capturing stunning skyline photos (*John Seigenthaler Pedestrian Bridge | Downtown Nashville*, n.d.). https://nashvilledowntown.com/go/shelby-street-pedestrian-bridge

Music City Walk of Fame - 121 4th Ave S: Located in a park across from the Country Music Hall of Fame, this landmark features star-studded plaques honoring artists from all genres who have contributed to Nashville's musical history. It's a FREE, must-see attraction for music lovers, celebrating the city's deep roots in country, rock, gospel, and beyond. www.visitmusiccity.com/walkoffame/

Tennessee State Capitol - 600 Dr. Martin Luther King Jr. Blvd: This historic landmark is one of the oldest working capitol buildings in the U.S. Designed by architect William Strickland and completed in 1859, this Greek Revival masterpiece sits atop Capitol Hill, offering stunning views of downtown Nashville. Visitors can explore its grand halls, learn about Tennessee's political history on guided tours, and see monuments honoring figures like President Andrew Jackson (*State Capitol | Tennessee State Museum*, n.d.). https://tnmuseum.org/state-capitol

The Belmont Mansion - 1700 Acklen Ave: A stunning antebellum home and one of Nashville's most beautifully preserved historic sites. Built in the mid-1800s by Adelicia Acklen, one of the wealthiest women of the era, the mansion showcases lavish Italianate architecture and ornate interiors. Visitors can take guided tours to learn about the home's history, its role during the Civil War, and the remarkable life of its owner. **Located on the Belmont University campus**, it's a must-see for history and architecture enthusiasts (*Belmont Mansion | Nashville Historic House Museum* |, n.d.). www.belmontmansion.com/

The General Jackson Showboat - 2812 Opryland Dr: One of the largest paddlewheel riverboats in the country, this showboat offers a unique way to experience Nashville. This iconic vessel cruises the Cumberland River, providing stunning skyline views, live entertainment, and delicious Southern cuisine. Guests can enjoy daytime and evening cruises featuring country, bluegrass, and rock music performances in a grand Victorian theater (*Nashville River Cruises | General Jackson Showboat*, 2023). https://generaljackson.com/

The Parthenon in Centennial Park - 2500 West End Ave: One of Nashville's most iconic landmarks, offering a **full-scale replica** of the ancient Greek masterpiece in Athens. Originally built for the 1897 Tennessee Centennial Exposition, **it now houses an impressive art museum and a 42-foot statue of Athena, the largest indoor sculpture in the Western Hemisphere**. Visitors can explore the museum's exhibits, admire classical architecture, enjoy candle-lit concerts, and stroll through the scenic park. A must-see attraction, it showcases why Nashville is known as the "Athens of the South" (*The Parthenon | Nashville's Full-scale Replica of the Greek Landmark*, n.d.). https://www.nashvilleparthenon.com/

Photo Credit: Sean Pavone – TN State Capitol Building

Photo Credit: Agnieszka – The Parthenon

11

WORLD FAMOUS MUSIC VENUES

Whether you prefer classic country, rock, or blues, catching a live show at one of Nashville's iconic music venues is the best way to dive into the city's legendary music scene.

NOTE: It is recommended that you purchase your tickets in advance.

The Bluebird Café - 4104 Hillsboro Pike: This cozy yet legendary café, featured on the TV show *Nashville*, has helped launch the careers of countless songwriters and artists, including Garth Brooks and Taylor Swift. With its "in-the-round" performances, where songwriters share their songs and stories, it gives you a one-of-a-kind, up-close look at Nashville's songwriting scene. With just 90 seats, getting in can be challenging, but it's well worth it for an unforgettable night of music.
For tickets: https://bluebirdcafe.com/

The Grand Ole Opry House—2804 Opryland Dr: This legendary venue, home of the world-famous **Grand Ole Opry** show, has hosted the biggest names in country music, from Hank Williams and Patsy Cline to today's top artists. Visitors can attend live Opry performances, take **behind-the-scenes tours**, and step onto the iconic stage. With its state-of-the-art sound and rich musical history, the Opry House offers a classic Nashville experience. **For tickets:** www.opry.com/

The Ryman - 116 5th Ave N: Known as the **"Mother Church of Country Music,"** this venue is one of the most iconic music venues in the world. Originally built as a tabernacle in 1892, this historic venue became home to the **Grand Ole Opry** from 1943 to 1974, hosting legends like Johnny Cash, Patsy Cline, and Elvis Presley. Today, the Ryman continues to welcome top artists from all genres, offering an intimate setting with incredible acoustics. Visitors can explore its rich history on guided tours or experience the magic of a live performance (Auditorium, n.d.). **For Tickets:** www.ryman.com/

The Station Inn—402 12th Ave South: This iconic establishment has been a staple in Nashville's music scene for over 40 years. It is recognized for its commitment to preserving the classic Nashville music tradition. This world-famous venue is known for classic bluegrass, roots, and Americana music and offers an intimate, down-home vibe. Seats are first-come, first-served. **For tickets:** http://stationinn.com/

12

MUSEUMS & THE ARTS

Discover Nashville's rich cultural scene by exploring its museums, theaters, and art galleries, where history and creativity come to life in every exhibit and performance.

Museums

Andrew Jackson's Presidential Museum — The Hermitage - 4580 Rachels Ln: A historic plantation and museum once the home of the seventh President of the United States, Andrew Jackson. The estate spans approximately 1,120 acres and includes more than 30 historic buildings, including the main mansion, restored slave cabins, and various outbuildings. Also on site is the **Natchez Hills Winery.** https://thehermitage.com/

Frist Art Museum - 919 Broadway: Located in a beautifully repurposed 1930s post office, the Frist Art Museum is Nashville's premier destination for visual arts. Unlike traditional museums, the Frist does not have a permanent collection but instead features rotating exhibitions from around the world, showcasing everything from classical masterpieces to contemporary works. https://fristartmuseum.org/

Johnny Cash Museum - 119 3rd Ave S: Dedicated to the "Man in Black," this museum houses the world's most extensive collection of Johnny Cash memorabilia. www.johnnycashmuseum.com/

Lane Motor Museum - 702 Murfreesboro Pike: Discover a unique collection of rare and quirky automobiles, motorcycles, and aeronautical artifacts from around the world. www.lanemotormuseum.org/

Marathon Motor Works Museum - 1305 Clinton St: Marathon Motor Works was Nashville's first and only early 20th-century automobile manufacturer, operating from 1907 to 1914 (*Marathon Village*, n.d.). Today, its historic factory buildings have been transformed into **Marathon Village**, a vibrant destination filled with shops, distilleries, and artisan studios. Visitors can explore the **Marathon Motor Works Museum**, which showcases vintage Marathon automobiles and tells the story of Nashville's industrial past. Located just northwest of downtown. https://marathonvillage.net/

Musicians Hall of Fame and Museum - 401 Gay St: Honoring musicians from all genres, this museum showcases the stories of studio musicians who have played on some of the greatest recordings of all time. www.musicianshalloffame.com/

National Museum of African American Music - 510 Broadway: The only museum in the nation dedicated to the impact of African American Music, spanning genres like blues, jazz, gospel, and hip-hop. USA Today named NMAAM the "Best New Museum in 2021" (*National Museum of*

MUSEUMS & THE ARTS

African American Music | Nashville, TN, n.d.). www.nmaam.org/

Patsy Cline Museum - 119 3rd Ave S: Celebrate the life and legacy of Patsy Cline with personal artifacts, costumes, and rare photographs. www.patsymuseum.com/

RCA Studio B - 1611 Roy Acuff PL: Experience the birthplace of the "Nashville Sound" with a tour of this historic recording studio where legends like Elvis Presley recorded hits. www.countrymusichalloffame.org/experiences/studio-b

Tennessee State Museum - 1000 Rosa L. Parks: Opened in 2018. Journey through Tennessee's history, from its prehistoric past to the present, with exhibits on the Civil War, civil rights, and more. **FREE! Kids love it.** https://tnmuseum.org/

Willie Nelson and Friends Museum - 2613 McGavock Pike: Right across from The Opryland Hotel, this museum takes you on a journey through country music history, with a huge collection of personal items and memorabilia from Willie Nelson and over 35 other legends, like Waylon Jennings, Hank Williams Jr., Dolly Parton, and Patsy Cline. Plus, visitors can check out Nashville's biggest souvenir shop while they're there. www.legendsofcountrymusic.com/

Theaters

Belcourt Theatre - 2102 Belcourt Ave: Nashville's historic independent cinema, offering a unique mix of classic, foreign, and indie films. Originally opened in 1925 as a silent movie house, it has since become a beloved cultural hub, hosting film screenings, special events, and educational programs. **For tickets:** www.belcourt.org/

Tennessee Performing Arts Center (TPAC) - 505 Deaderick St: Nashville's premier venue for live theater, Broadway productions, concerts, and cultural performances. Located in the heart of downtown, TPAC houses multiple theaters, including Andrew Jackson Hall, James K. Polk Theater, and the intimate Andrew Johnson Theater. The center hosts national touring shows, ballet, opera, and performances by local arts organizations like the Nashville Repertory Theatre. Whether you're catching a Broadway hit or a homegrown production, TPAC offers world-class entertainment in Music City. **For tickets**: www.tpac.org/events

Art Galleries

5th Avenue of the Arts: Situated along 5th Avenue North, this area is renowned for its concentration of contemporary art galleries. The district offers a diverse array of art exhibitions featuring works from both local and international artists. A highlight of this area is the **Second Saturday Art Crawl.** In this monthly event, galleries extend their hours, allowing visitors to explore exhibitions, meet artists, and enjoy the local art scene. The district's proximity to other downtown attractions makes it a must-visit destination for art enthusiasts. https://nashvilledowntown.com/go/5th-avenue-of-the-arts

Chauvet Art Gallery - 215 Rep. John Lewis Way N: This gallery spans over 4,000 square feet within a historic building on the renowned 5th Avenue of the Arts. Chauvet Arts specializes in distinctive artwork from top local and regional artists, focusing on styles and stories that capture the authenticity of the American South (*Home*, n.d.).

Haley Art Gallery - 224 Rep John Lewis Way S: An art space associated with the Country Music Hall of Fame® and Museum. A portion of proceeds from artwork purchased in the gallery supports the nonprofit museum's educational mission. **FREE** and open to the public. https://haleyartgallery.com/

Tinney Contemporary Art Gallery - 237 5th Ave N: Specializes in established artists' collectible contemporary works. The gallery focuses on painting, photography, sculpture, and installation-based work. https://tinneycontemporary.com/

Art Crawls

Nashville's vibrant art scene is showcased through tours and several monthly art crawls:

FirstBank First Saturday Art Crawl: Held on the **first Saturday of each month from 5:00 PM to 8:00 PM in downtown Nashville**, this event features numerous galleries presenting diverse exhibitions. Attendees can explore a variety of artworks, often accompanied by light refreshments. The event is **FREE** and open to the public. https://nashvilledowntown.com/do/firstbank-first-saturday-art-crawl

Second Saturday Art Crawl: Organized by the Downtown Art District Association, this **FREE** event occurs on the **second Saturday of each month from 6:00 PM to 9:00 PM**. Galleries in the downtown area showcase new exhibitions, providing an opportunity for art enthusiasts to engage with the local art scene. https://nashvilledowntown.com/do/artist-talk-and-walk-dada-nashville-second-saturday-art-crawl

Street Art Mural Tour - Nashville's vibrant street art scene offers visitors a unique way to explore the city's culture through its colorful and iconic murals. A number of tour operators offer fun guided tours to explore Nashville's vibrant street art scene, like the **Nashville Mural Tour, Joyride's Mural and Instagram Tour on golf carts, and Mint Julep's Murals & Mimosas Tour**. If you'd rather go at your own pace, the 12 South neighborhood is a must-see, with its collection of stunning murals, including the famous "I Believe in Nashville" mural. www.visit musiccity.com/nashville-trip-ideas/nashville-murals

WEHO Art Crawl: Taking place on the **first Saturday of each month in the Wedgewood-Houston neighborhood**, this crawl invites visitors to immerse themselves in Nashville's creative community. Approximately a dozen art spaces open their doors, offering a range of artistic expressions. While the event is **FREE**, checking individual gallery schedules is advisable, as hours may vary. www.wehoartsnashville.com/

* * *

Museums & Tours already mentioned in previous chapters:

- Belle Meade Plantation
- Belmont Mansion
- Cheekwood Botanical Garden and Museum
- Country Music Hall of Fame and Museum
- The Parthenon
- The Ryman Tour
- The Tennessee State Capitol

13

LARGE CONCERT & EVENT VENUES

Experience the thrill of live music in Nashville by attending a concert at one of the city's premier venues, where world-class artists take the stage.

NOTE: It is recommended that you purchase your tickets in advance.

Ascend Amphitheater - 310 1st Ave S: Located along the Cumberland River, Ascend Amphitheater is a state-of-the-art outdoor music venue in downtown Nashville. With breathtaking skyline views and a capacity of 6,800, this open-air venue hosts top artists across all genres, from country and rock to pop and indie. The Amphitheater offers both reserved seating and spacious lawn areas. Ascend Amphitheater is one of the best places to enjoy live music under the stars in Music City. **For upcoming events and tickets: www.ascendamphitheater.com**

Bridgestone Arena - 501 Broadway: The arena has hosted various events, including major concerts, family shows, and sporting events.

The arena is also **home to the NHL's Nashville Predators**. With a seating capacity of up to 20,000, it offers attendees an intimate yet electrifying atmosphere. **For upcoming events and tickets: www.bridgestonearena.com**

Nissan Stadium - 1 Titans Way: Located along the Cumberland River, Nissan Stadium is a premier venue for large-scale concerts, festivals, and major events in Nashville. With a seating capacity of nearly 70,000, this open-air stadium is **home to the Tennessee Titans** but also hosts top-tier concerts from global superstars, including Taylor Swift, Beyoncé, and the Rolling Stones. This venue is also a key location for massive music festivals like the CMA Fest. **For upcoming events and tickets: www.nissanstadium.com**

GEODIS Park Soccer Stadium - 501 Benton Ave: With a seating capacity of 30,000, Nashville's newest state-of-the-art sports and entertainment venue is located in the Wedgewood-Houston neighborhood. Primarily serving as **the home of Nashville SC**, the city's Major League Soccer team, the venue features modern amenities, including multiple lounges and premium seating options. ****TIP:** Use a ride-share service, as parking can be difficult. **For upcoming events and tickets: www.geodispark.com**

The Schermerhorn Symphony Center - 1 Symphony Place: A premier concert hall in downtown Nashville's SoBro district. **Home to the GRAMMY® Award-winning Nashville Symphony**, the center hosts over 140 events annually, encompassing classical, pop, jazz, and family concerts and performances by visiting artists across various musical genres (*Nashville Symphony*, n.d.). **For upcoming events and tickets: www.nashvillesymphony.org**

LARGE CONCERT & EVENT VENUES

Skydeck - 5055 Broadway Place: Nashville's **largest rooftop patio and concert venue,** located on the third floor of Assembly Food Hall within the Fifth + Broadway development. With a capacity of up to 1,600 guests, visitors can enjoy live music, diverse dining options from over 20 eateries, and panoramic views of downtown Nashville. **For upcoming events and tickets: www.assemblyfoodhall.com/skydeck/**

Musicians Corner - 2500 West End Ave: A **FREE,** family-friendly concert series held in **Centennial Park** during the spring and fall. Attendees can enjoy live music from diverse artists, food trucks, local artisans, and a Kidsville activity area. The event is pet-friendly, with water stations available for leashed dogs. **For upcoming events and tickets: www.musicianscornernashville.com**

Candlelight Concert Series - 2500 West End Ave: Inside the iconic Parthenon in Centennial Park. These unique performances feature live musicians illuminated by candlelight, creating an intimate and memorable atmosphere beneath the 42-foot statue of Athena. The series offers diverse musical tributes, including classical masterpieces and contemporary favorites. **For upcoming events and tickets: www.conservancyonline.com/events**

Marathon Music Works - 1402 Clinton St: Originally built in the early 1900s as an auto manufacturing plant, the venue has been transformed into a 14,000-square-foot space that blends industrial chic design with modern amenities. With a standing room capacity of 1,800, it offers an intimate yet energetic atmosphere for a variety of performances and events (Marathon Music Works, 2024). **For upcoming events and tickets: www.marathonmusicworks.com**

* * *

Large concert venues already mentioned in a previous chapter:

- The Ryman Auditorium – 116 Rep. John Lewis Way: www.ryman.com
- The Grand Ole Opry – 600 Opry Mills Drive: www.opry.com

Photo Credit: Jejim – Grand Ole Opry House Stage

IV

BRUNCH, LIQUID GOLD, & SHOPPING

14

POPULAR BRUNCH SPOTS

Please note that brunch hours can vary, especially on weekends. It's advisable to check with each restaurant for their current hours and reservation policies.

Downtown

- **417 Union** (casual) – Thursday thru Monday
- **Acme Feed & Seed** (1st Floor) – Saturdays only **with live blues music**
- **Another Broken Egg Cafe** – seven days a week
- **Boqueria** – Friday thru Sunday
- **Cafe Intermezzo** (casual) – seven days a week
- **Church and Union** – Friday thru Sunday
- **City Winery** – weekends only
- **Frothy Monkey** (casual) – seven days a week
- **Gray & Dudley** (Printer's Alley) – weekends only
- **Husk** – weekends only
- **Liberty Common** – Thursday thru Sunday

- **Pinewood Social** - Friday thru Sunday
- **Sinatra Bar & Lounge** (Printer's Alley) - Sundays only
- **Sixty Vines** - weekends only
- **Skull's Rainbow Room** (Printer's Alley) - Sundays only **with live Jazz music**
- **Stateside Kitchen at Dream Hotel** (reservations recommended) - upscale with a DJ - Friday thru Sunday
- **Sun Diner** - seven days a week
- **The Farm House** - weekends only
- **The Goat** - weekends only
- **The Hampton Social (Rooftop)** - weekends only **with live music**
- **The Listening Room** - Saturdays only **with live music**
- **The Pancake Pantry** (casual) - seven days a week
- **Tin Roof** - **with live music** on weekends only
- **Twelve Thirty Club's Honky Tonk** (1st Floor) - seven days a week **with live music**
- **Twelve Thirty Club (Rooftop)** - weekends only

East Nashville

- **Butcher & Bee** - weekends only
- **Café Roze** - seven days a week
- **East Park Donuts & Coffee** - seven days a week
- **Frothy Monkey** (casual) - seven days a week
- **Graze Nashville (Vegan)** - seven days a week
- **Hearts** - seven days a week
- **Margot Cafe & Bar** - Sundays only
- **Shugga Hi Bakery and Cafe** - Sundays only **with live jazz music**
- **Sky Blue Cafe** - seven days a week
- **SweetMilk** - Monday thru Friday
- **The Treehouse Restaurant** - weekends only

POPULAR BRUNCH SPOTS

- **Yeast Nashville** – seven days a week

Germantown

- **Butchertown Hall** – Friday thru Sunday
- **Germantown Café** – weekends only (with panoramic views of downtown)
- **Henrietta Red** – weekends only
- **Monell's Dining & Catering** – weekends only
- **Mother's Ruin** – seven days a week
- **The Goat** – weekends only
- **The Red Bicycle** – weekends only
- **Von Elrods Beer Hall & Kitchen** – weekends only

The Gulch

- **Adeles** – weekends only
- **Bar Louie** – Friday thru Sunday
- **Biscuit Love** – seven days a week
- **Emmy Squared Pizza** – weekends only
- **LA Jackson (Rooftop)** – Sundays only
- **Milk & Honey** – seven days a week
- **Party Fowl** – seven days a week
- **Sambuca Restaurant** – Friday thru Sunday **with live music**
- **Snooze AM Eatery** – seven days a week
- **Stompin Grounds** – weekends only
- **Sunda** – weekends only

Midtown, Music Row, and West End

- **Amerigo Italian Restaurant** – weekends only
- **Barcelona Wine Bar** – weekends only
- **ButterFLY Garden Brunch** – offers a bottomless brunch experience. They have been hosting their exclusive bottomless brunch at **Jar10 Nashville,** a Hookah bar in the Hillsboro Village area – weekends only
- **Elliston Place Soda Shop** – breakfast daily and brunch on Sundays only
- **Halls Chophouse** – Sundays only
- **Hattie B's Hot Chicken** (Midtown location only): Sundays only
- **HiFi Clyde's Nashville** – brunch all day, Tuesday thru Sunday
- **Jasper's** – Friday thru Monday
- **Mason's at Loews Vanderbilt Hotel** – weekends only
- **Suzy Wong's House of Yum Drag 'N Brunch** – brunch **with a drag show,** Friday thru Sunday. **Reservations are suggested**: www.suzywongsnashville.com/
- **Tavern Nashville** – Friday thru Sunday
- **The Butter Milk Ranch** – chef-driven brunch Tuesday through Sunday (located in the 12South neighborhood a short distance east of West End and south of Music Row. A favorite of locals and too good not to include!)
- **The Electric Jane** – Saturdays only
- **The Local** – Friday thru Sunday
- **The Mockingbird** – Wednesday thru Sunday
- **The Pool Club at Virgin Hotel (Rooftop)** – Friday thru Sunday
- **The Row Kitchen & Pub** – seven days a week

15

LIQUID GOLD

Music City Brew Hop

Nashville's top hop-on, hop-off brewery tour is a fun and easy way to check out the city's booming craft beer scene. The trolley-style bus takes you to some of the best local breweries, with stops in East Nashville, Germantown, and The Gulch. With the flexibility to explore at your own pace, guests can sample local brews, enjoy brewery tours, and soak in Music City's craft beer culture. **To book a ticket:** www.musiccitybrewhop.com

Tennessee Whiskey Tours

Guests can visit world-renowned distilleries like Jack Daniel's, George Dickel, and smaller craft producers with guided tours departing from Nashville. Along the way, expert guides offer interesting stories about Tennessee whiskey's history, craftsmanship, and distinctive flavors. Whether you opt for a half-day, full-day, or private tour, you'll enjoy tastings, behind-the-scenes access, and a scenic ride through the beautiful rolling hills of middle Tennessee's whiskey country. **To book a ticket:** www.tennesseewhiskeytours.com

Breweries and Distilleries

Check out the taprooms at the various local breweries. Each one is distinct, and they often demo new recipes. If you see something unique... Try it! You may never see that flavor again.

Jack Daniel's Distillery

Jack Daniel's Distillery - 280 Lynchburg Hwy, Lynchburg, TN 37352: One of the most iconic whiskey distilleries in the world, located in the charming town of **Lynchburg, Tennessee**, about 90 minutes south of Nashville. As the home of the legendary Jack Daniel's Tennessee Whiskey, this historic distillery offers guided tours where visitors can learn about the time-honored charcoal mellowing process, explore the barrel houses, and sample a variety of signature whiskeys. www.jackdaniels.com/en-us/visit-distillery

Downtown

6th & Peabody - 423 6th Ave S - Downtown Nashville: A lively entertainment venue that is a **distillery and brewery combo**! This popular locale offers a wide selection of house-made beers, Tennessee whiskey, moonshine tastings, and classic Southern bites from White Duck Taco and Daddy's Dogs. With a **spacious beer garden, live music, and big-screen TVs** for game days, **6th & Peabody** is the perfect family-friendly place to relax and soak in the Music City vibe. https://6thandpeabody.com/ **This hotspot is the home to:**

- **Ole Smoky Distillery**: As one of the most popular distilleries in the state, Ole Smoky offers visitors the chance to sample a variety of handcrafted moonshines and whiskeys, from classic White Lightning to unique flavors like Apple Pie and Peanut Butter Whiskey. Enjoy live music, outdoor games, and a welcoming beer garden shared with Yee-Haw Brewing Co.
- **Yee-Haw Brewing Co.**: Known for its bold, flavorful beers, Yee-Haw offers a wide selection of lagers, IPAs, porters, and seasonal brews. The taproom and spacious outdoor beer garden provide the perfect setting to enjoy a cold pint.

Big Machine Brewery and Distillery - 122 3rd Ave S: A one-of-a-kind destination in Downtown Nashville, offering **both handcrafted spirits and locally brewed beers.** Home to **Big Machine Vodka**, this popular spot features a full-service bar, signature cocktails, and tasting flights of its award-winning spirits. Beer lovers can also enjoy a rotating selection of craft brews made on-site. Has **live music**, a vibrant atmosphere, and a prime location near Broadway. www.bigmachinevodka.com/

Tennessee Brew Works - 809 Ewing Ave: Known for its signature brews like the State Park Blonde Ale and Southern Wit, this brewery uses Tennessee-sourced ingredients to create distinct, flavorful beers. The inviting taproom **features live music, a rooftop patio, and a full kitchen** serving Southern-inspired dishes designed to pair perfectly with their brews. www.tnbrew.com/

East Nashville

Crazy Gnome Brewery - 948 Main St: Known for its crisp lagers, hoppy IPAs, and refreshing sours, this independent brewery offers a laid-back atmosphere with a spacious patio perfect for enjoying a pint. www.cgbrewing.com/

East Nashville Beer Works - 320 E Trinity Ln: This brewery features a spacious taproom, a large outdoor beer garden, and a nice **family-friendly playground**. A community-focused brewery known for its easy-drinking, well-balanced craft beers and welcoming atmosphere. https://eastnashbeerworks.com/

Living Waters Brewery - 1056 E Trinity Ln: A unique craft brewery and coffee bar. Known for its meticulously crafted stouts, lagers, and IPAs, this small-batch brewery focuses on high-quality ingredients and bold flavors. https://livingwatersbrewing.com/

Nashville Barrel Company - 809 Fesslers Ln: A craft whiskey distillery specializing in high-quality, single-barrel bourbon and rye. This boutique distillery offers a personalized whiskey experience, allowing visitors to explore unique barrel-aged selections and even participate in custom barrel picks. The tasting room provides an intimate setting to sample expertly crafted spirits while learning about the art of whiskey blending and aging. www.nashvillebarrelco.com/

Southern Grist Brewery- 754 Douglas Ave: Known for its bold and innovative brews, this locally loved brewery pushes the boundaries of traditional beer styles with unique flavor combinations and experimental ingredients. www.southerngristbrewing.com/

TailGate Brewery East Nashville—811 Gallatin Ave: This location features a spacious taproom and outdoor seating. It offers a rotating lineup of IPAs, stouts, sours, and creative seasonal brews. In addition to great beer, TailGate is known for its delicious pizza, making it a perfect stop for a laid-back hangout. www.southerngristbrewing.com/

Marathon Village

Nelson's Green Brier Distillery - 1414 Clinton St: A historic whiskey distillery just northwest of downtown revives the legacy of one of Tennessee's original pre-prohibition whiskey brands. Founded in the 1800s and brought back to life by the Nelson family, this distillery offers guided tours showcasing its rich history, traditional production methods, and the craftsmanship behind its award-winning Belle Meade Bourbon and Tennessee whiskey (*Nelson's Green Brier Distillery | Nelson's Green Brier Distillery*, n.d.). https://greenbrierdistillery.com/

Wedgewood-Houston Neighborhood

Corsair Artisan Distillery - 601 Merritt Ave: Known for its bold whiskey and gin-making approach. This award-winning distillery experiments with unique grains, smoked malts, and barrel-aging techniques to create one-of-a-kind spirits. Visitors can take a guided tour to learn about the distillation process and sample small-batch whiskeys. www.corsairdistillery.com/marathon/

Diskin Cider - 1235 Martin St: Nashville's first and only craft cidery, bringing a fresh, modern twist to traditional cider-making. For a refreshing alternative to beer, this locally loved cidery offers a variety of all-natural, gluten-free ciders made with fresh-pressed apples— no artificial flavors or added sugars. The taproom features a rotating selection of innovative ciders, seasonal releases, and craft cocktails, all served in a welcoming, industrial-chic space. Enjoy **live music**, delicious food, and a **dog-friendly patio**. www.diskincider.com/

Jackalope Brewing Company - 429B Houston St: As one of Nashville's first female-founded breweries, Jackalope offers a diverse lineup of year-round and seasonal brews, including their popular Bearwalker Maple Brown Ale and Thunder Ann American Pale Ale. The spacious "The Ranch" taproom provides a cozy atmosphere, while the outdoor patio is perfect for relaxing with friends. https://jackalopebrew.com/

The Nations Neighborhood

Fat Bottom Brewing Co - 800 44th Ave N: This brewery offers a diverse selection of lagers, IPAs, porters, and seasonal brews, all crafted with quality ingredients and creativity. The spacious taproom features a welcoming atmosphere, while the outdoor beer garden provides the perfect setting to enjoy a pint with friends. Has a full-service kitchen serving up delicious pub fare. www.fatbottombrewing.com/

Vineyards & Wineries

Arrington Vineyards and Winery - 6211 Patton Rd, Arrington, TN 37014: A picturesque winery located in the rolling hills of Arrington, Tennessee, just **30 minutes south of Nashville.** Co-owned by country music star Kix Brooks, this award-winning vineyard is the perfect spot for a peaceful getaway. With breathtaking views, handcrafted wines, and a laid-back vibe, it offers a truly relaxing experience. Guests can enjoy wine tastings, hang out in picnic areas, and catch live music on weekends. https://arringtonvineyards.com/ **Food options for visitors:**

- **Picnic-Friendly** – Guests are welcome to bring their own food and enjoy a picnic on the scenic vineyard grounds.
- **Food Trucks** – On weekends, Arrington features a rotating selection of food trucks offering various options, from barbecue to gourmet snacks.
- **Cheese & Charcuterie** – The **Vineyard House** sells a selection of **cheese, meats, crackers, and other picnic-friendly snacks** that pair well with their wines.

Belle Meade Winery - 5025 Harding Pike, Nashville, TN 37205: Located on the Belle Meade Historic Site & Mansion grounds, this winery was established to continue the property's long winemaking tradition. The winery specializes in handcrafted reds, whites, and dessert wines. Visitors can enjoy guided wine tastings, explore the historic grounds, and pair their wine with a bourbon-tasting experience. www.bellemeadewinery.com/ **Food Options for visitors:**

- **Gourmet Cheese & Charcuterie Boards** – Available for wine tastings featuring artisan cheeses, meats, crackers, and fruit.
- **Picnic-Style Snacks** – Light bites and packaged snacks are available for purchase and enjoyment on the grounds.
- **The Belle Meade Meat & Three** – Located on-site, this Southern-style eatery serves hearty dishes like fried chicken, BBQ, and classic sides, perfect for pairing with a glass of wine.

City Winery - 609 Lafayette - Downtown: A unique urban **winery, restaurant, and live music venue** in the **heart of downtown Nashville**. Combining a love for wine, gourmet dining, and live entertainment, this stylish venue offers a diverse selection of house-made wines crafted on-site alongside a globally inspired, wine-paired cuisine menu. Guests can enjoy intimate concerts, wine tastings, and even wine-blending experiences, all in a chic yet relaxed setting. https://citywinery.com/nashville

Grinder's Switch Winery: A charming, family-owned winery with a welcoming, rustic atmosphere offering handcrafted Tennessee wines. The winery's main vineyard and tasting room are located in **Centerville, Tennessee,** about **an hour west of Nashville,** while its **Nashville tasting room is conveniently located in Marathon Village.** Visitors can sample various wines, from dry reds and whites to sweet Southern-style muscadine and fruit wines. https://gswinery.com/ **Food options for visitors:**

- **Picnic-Friendly at the Vineyard** – Guests can bring their own food to enjoy on the scenic winery grounds.
- **Charcuterie & Cheese Boards** – Available at the Nashville tasting room, featuring artisan meats, cheeses, and crackers.
- **Nearby Marathon Village Eateries** – The Nashville location is surrounded by local food spots where guests can grab a bite before or after their wine tasting.

📍 **Vineyard & Main Winery Address**: 2119 Hwy 50 W, Centerville, TN 37033

📍 **Nashville Tasting Room Address**: inside Marathon Village, 1310 Clinton St, Suite 125, Nashville, TN 37203

Love and Exile Bar - 715 Main St - East Nashville: Produces its wines on-site, offering a selection of house-made reds, whites, and rosés in a relaxed, modern setting. **In addition to wine, the bar serves craft cocktails and beer**, making it a versatile spot for all drink lovers. This winery, bar, and lounge offer a stylish atmosphere, cozy patio, and welcoming vibe. www.loveandexile.bar/ **Food options for visitors:**

- **Light Bites & Snacks** – A rotating menu of small plates and shareable snacks.
- **Charcuterie & Cheese Boards** – Available to pair with house wines.
- **Nearby East Nashville Restaurants** – Located close to various dining options for a full night out.

Natchez Hills Vineyard & Winery: A boutique, family-owned winery offering an authentic taste of Tennessee with handcrafted, old-world-style wines. Located one hour south of Nashville in **Hampshire, Tennessee**, visitors can tour the winery, enjoy guided tastings, and sip on bold reds, crisp whites, and sweet muscadine wines. For those exploring Nashville, Natchez Hills Winery has **two convenient tasting rooms**: one at **Andrew Jackson's Hermitage,** where guests can enjoy wine while immersing themselves in Tennessee history, and **The Nashville Farmers' Market** if you want to stay downtown. www.natchezhills.com/ **Food Options at Natchez Hills Winery Locations:**

- **Light Snacks & Wine Pairings** – Available at all tasting rooms.
- **Picnic-Friendly at the Vineyard & Hermitage** – Guests can bring their own food to enjoy with wine.
- **Nashville Farmers' Market Vendors** – Various food options surround the downtown tasting room.

📍 **Main Winery & Vineyard:** 109 Overhead Bridge Rd, Hampshire, TN 38461

📍 **Tasting Room at The Hermitage:** 4580 Rachel's Lane, Nashville, TN 37076

📍 **Tasting Room at The Nashville Farmers' Market:** 900 Rosa L. Parks Blvd, Nashville, TN 37208

16

SHOPPING

Nashville offers a diverse shopping scene, from high-end boutiques to local artisan markets. Here are some of the best shopping destinations:

Boutiques & Fashion

12South District: A trendy area with stylish boutiques like Draper James (Reese Witherspoon's brand), Imogene + Willie (handcrafted denim), and White's Mercantile (modern general store).

Hillsboro Village: A charming shopping area with unique finds like Posh Boutique and Revival Nashville.

The Gulch Neighborhood: One of Nashville's trendiest shopping districts, The Gulch is home to Lucchese Bootmaker, Kittenish, e.Allen, Blush, Parish, and other upscale fashion and lifestyle stores.

Vintage & Local Finds

Fatherland District (East Nashville): Features a mix of vintage, handmade, and indie shops like The Soda Parlor and Rusty Rats Antiques. The district is located **between 10th and 11th Streets along Fatherland Street**, near the trendy **Five Points** area. www.fatherlanddistrict.com/

Garage Sale Vintage & Bar - 5040 Broadway (Downtown **inside 5th + Broadway**): This eclectic venue offers a curated selection of vintage clothing, accessories, and vinyl records. While browsing, guests can enjoy **handcrafted cocktails** and indulge in **street tacos**. The space also features **retro games** like pinball. https://garagesalevintage.com/

Hip Zipper - 1008 Forrest Ave (East Nashville): A must-visit for vintage lovers searching for curated retro clothing. https://hipzipper.com/

Marathon Village - 1305 Clinton St (Downtown): A historic factory turned shopping hub with local brands like Grinder's Switch Winery, Jack Daniel's General Store, and Nashville Olive Oil Co. https://marathonvillage.net/

Starland Vintage & Unusual - 2110 8th Ave S (West End near Belmont University): This hidden gem offers a carefully curated selection of vintage clothing, accessories, collectibles, and oddities, making it a must-visit for those looking for one-of-a-kind finds. www.yelp.com/biz/starland-vintage-and-unusual-nashville-4

Music & Memorabilia

Carter Vintage Guitars - 625 8th Ave S (Downtown): A must-visit for music lovers looking for rare and high-end guitars. https://cartervintage.com/

Ernest Tubb Record Shop - 417 Broadway (Downtown): One of Nashville's most iconic record shops for country music lovers. www.ernesttubbrecordshop.co/

Grimey's New & Preloved Music - 1060 East Trinity Lane (East Nashville): This independent record store is known for its vast selection of new and used albums, rare finds, vinyl records, CDs, cassettes, live in-store music, and a welcoming community vibe. www.grimeys.com/

Third Man Records - 621 7th Ave S (Downtown): Founded by Jack White, this shop offers vinyl records, rare collectibles, a recording booth, and live in-store performances. https://thirdmanrecords.com/

Markets & Artisan Goods

Made in Tennessee - 2 locations (Downtown): A store dedicated to locally made gifts, food items, and souvenirs. https://shopmadeintn.com/

- **Nashville Farmers' Market - 900 Rosa L Parks Blvd** - inside the Market House Building.
- **L&L Market - 3820 Charlotte Ave** - located in **The Nations** neighborhood on the city's west side.

The Nashville Farmers' Market - 900 Rosa L Parks Blvd (Downtown):

SHOPPING

Located near **Germantown** and **Bicentennial Capitol Mall State Park**, the Nashville Farmers' Market is a year-round marketplace featuring local produce, artisan goods, international eateries, and specialty shops. It's a great spot to experience Nashville's diverse food scene and shop for unique, locally made products! www.nashvillefarmersmarket.org/

The Shoppes on Fatherland - 1006 Fatherland St (East Nashville): A collection of small boutiques featuring handmade jewelry, home goods, gifts, apparel, and more, all housed in a walkable, village-style setting. www.fatherlanddistrict.com/

Uncommon James - 601 9th Ave S (The Gulch): This boutique, founded by Kristin Cavallari, features minimalist jewelry, home goods, and accessories, many locally crafted. https://uncommonjames.com/

Shopping Malls & Outlets

5th + Broadway - 500 Broadway (Downtown): This vibrant mixed-use complex offers an exciting mix of high-end and local retail shops, diverse restaurants, and live entertainment venues, all just steps away from Broadway's famous honky-tonks. Visitors can shop at national brands and unique Nashville-based stores, enjoy world-class dining, and explore the **National Museum of African American Music** housed within the development. Shop stores like Vera Bradley, Lululemon, Nike, Apple, Carhartt, and so much MORE! https://fifthandb.com/

L&L Market - 3820 Charlotte Ave (The Nations neighborhood): A stylish indoor market housed in a beautifully restored warehouse, this shopping and dining destination features a curated selection of **local boutiques, artisan shops, specialty food vendors, and wellness studios**. Whether you're looking for unique home décor, trendy fashion, handcrafted gifts, or a great cup of coffee, L&L Market offers a one-of-a-kind shopping experience in a relaxed, modern setting. https://landlmarket.com/

Opry Mills Mall - 433 Opry Mills Dr (Opryland Area): Tennessee's largest **outlet and value retail shopping** destination with **over 200 stores**, offering Nike, Coach, Kate Spade, H&M, Michael Kors, and Bass Pro Shops, plus an IMAX theater and dining options. www.simon.com/mall/opry-mills

The Mall at Green Hills - 2126 Abbott Martin Rd (Green Hills Neighborhood): Nashville's **premier luxury shopping** destination, offering an upscale mix of designer brands, high-end department stores, and stylish boutiques. Located just a short drive from downtown Nashville, this elegant shopping center provides a refined atmosphere with top-tier fashion, beauty, and home décor retailers - featuring Louis Vuitton, Tiffany & Co., Apple, Nordstrom, Gucci, and MORE. https://shopgreenhills.com/

V

ANNUAL EVENTS & THINGS-TO-DO

17

FESTIVALS & ANNUAL EVENTS

Nashville has year-round festivals and events, making it a lively destination no matter what season you visit!

Music Festivals & Concert Events

AmericanaFest (September) – A **week-long celebration** of folk, bluegrass, and country music featuring industry panels and live performances. https://americanamusic.org/americanafest/

Bourbon & Bubbles Fest (April) - Combines tastings of bourbon, champagne, wine, and other spirits with live music and a fashion show. Held at Iroquois Steeplechase. www.bourbonbubblesfest.com/

Bonnaroo Music & Arts Festival (June) – A **legendary camping and music festival** in nearby **Manchester, TN**, featuring top international acts. www.bonnaroo.com/

CMA Fest (June) – The **biggest country music festival** in the world, featuring top artists performing across multiple stages in Downtown Nashville. https://cmafest.com/

Live on the Green (August-September) – **A free outdoor music festival** at Public Square Park featuring national and local artists. https://liveonthegreen.com/

Nashville Comedy Festival (April) - Features top comedians from around the world, bringing stand-up performances, improv shows, and celebrity acts to iconic venues across Music City. www.nashcomedyfest.com/

Pilgrimage Music & Cultural Festival (September) – A multi-genre festival held in **Franklin, TN**, featuring **rock, country, and indie artists**. https://pilgrimagefestival.com/

Tin Pan South Songwriters Festival (March) – The **largest songwriter festival**, showcasing legendary and up-and-coming songwriters in intimate venues all over town. www.tinpansouth.com/

Cultural & Food Festivals

Cherry Blossom Festival (April) - Held at **Public Square Park**, celebrates Japanese culture and the arrival of spring. Kicks off with the **Cherry Blossom Walk**, followed by a day filled with **traditional music and dance performances, martial arts demonstrations, cultural exhibits, and delicious Japanese cuisine** from local food vendors. www.nashvillecherryblossomfestival.org/

Light the Nations (October) - In **The Nations** neighborhood, this festival illuminates the area with local art, live music, food trucks, and family-friendly activities, showcasing the vibrant community spirit. www.lightthenationsnashville.com/

Music City Food + Wine Festival (April) – A premier **food and wine** event featuring celebrity chefs, tastings, and live entertainment. Held in **Centennial Park.** www.conservancyonline.com/events/music-city-food-and-wine-festival

Nashville Film Festival (September-October) – One of the **longest-running film festivals** in the U.S., showcasing independent films and documentaries in various theaters around Nashville. https://nashvillefilmfestival.org/

Nashville Oktoberfest (October): Held in the historic **Germantown** neighborhood, this festival is Nashville's oldest annual event. It celebrates German culture with traditional music, authentic cuisine, a beer garden, and the popular Dachshund Derby. www.visitmusiccity.com/nashville-events/oktoberfest

Nashville Pride Festival (June) - Tennessee's largest LGBTQ+ celebration, featuring a vibrant parade, live music, drag performances, and community events. Held at **Bicentennial Capitol Mall State Park.** www.nashvillepride.org/

Tomato Art Fest (August) – A quirky and popular **East Nashville tradition** celebrating art, music, and everything tomato-themed. www.tomatoartfest.com/

Seasonal & Holiday Events

Cheekwood Holiday Lights (November-December) – A dazzling **Christmas light display** at Cheekwood Estate & Gardens. https://cheekwood.org/tickets/

Let Freedom Sing! (July 4th) – Nashville's **massive Independence Day celebration** featuring fireworks and live music. www.nashville.com/event/music-citys-4th-of-july-let-freedom-sing-nashville-tn/

Opryland's A Country Christmas (November-December) – A spectacular **holiday event at Gaylord Opryland** featuring lights, ice displays, and themed entertainment. https://christmasatgaylordopryland.marriott.com/

Nashville's New Year's Eve Party - one of the biggest New Year's celebrations in the country, featuring live music, a massive fireworks display, **and the signature Music Note Drop** at midnight. www.visitmusiccity.com/newyearseve

Ryman New Year's Eve Concert (December 31st) – A **special New Year's Eve show** at the historic Ryman Auditorium. www.ryman.com/

Marathons & Races

Iroquois Steeplechase (May) – A **prestigious horse race** and social event held at Percy Warner Park. www.iroquoissteeplechase.org/

Music City July 4th 5K (July) - This race winds through downtown, allowing participants to experience the festive atmosphere of Independence Day in Music City. www.runnash.com/events/music-city-july-

FESTIVALS & ANNUAL EVENTS

4th-5k/

Nashville Half Marathon & 5K (October) - This race takes runners through downtown Nashville, experiencing the city's vibrant neighborhoods and scenic views. www.runnash.com/events/nashville-half-marathon/

Rock 'n' Roll Nashville Marathon (April) – A **scenic race through Music City** featuring live bands along the course. www.runrocknroll.com/nashville

Photo Credit: inhaus creative – New Year's Eve, Downtown Nashville, TN

18

UNIQUE THINGS-TO-DO

Nashville offers endless unique experiences, making it an exciting city for everyone! Here are a few ideas:

Adventure Science Center - 800 Fort Negley Blvd: The science center features over **175 hands-on exhibits** that explore topics such as biology, physics, earth science, and space. A highlight is the **Sudekum Planetarium**, a state-of-the-art 63-foot dome theater offering immersive shows about the cosmos (Adventure Science Center, 2025). The center also hosts various programs for all ages, including camps, workshops, and special events. www.adventuresci.org/

Backstage Nashville - 818 3rd Ave S: An intimate, one-of-a-kind live music experience that gives guests a behind-the-scenes look at **Music City's legendary songwriters**. Hosted at **3rd & Lindsley**, this **daytime songwriters' showcase** features Grammy-winning artists and hit songwriters performing the songs they wrote for some of country music's biggest stars. With personal storytelling and a relaxed, up-close atmosphere, this is a must-do for anyone wanting to experience Nashville's authentic music scene beyond the honky-tonks. www.backstagenashville.net/

Big Band Dance - 2500 West End Ave: Series during the summer months at **Centennial Park**. This **FREE**, family-friendly event features live music from **local swing and jazz big bands and complimentary dance lessons**. It is held in June through July each year, with dance lessons starting at 7:00 PM and live music at 7:30 PM. The dances are held at the Centennial Park Bandshell. www.conservancyonline.com/events/bigbanddances

Candlelight Music Concerts at The Parthenon - 2500 West End Ave: Experience enchanting **Candlelight Concerts** inside **The Parthenon**, where the warm glow of candles illuminates the iconic replica of the ancient Greek temple. These intimate performances feature talented musicians performing various genres, from classical masterpieces to contemporary favorites, all within the Parthenon's majestic setting. www.conservancyonline.com/events/fever-candlelight-concerts

Decorate and Design Your Own Cowboy Hat: Nashville is known for its **iconic cowboy hats**, and now you can customize your own! Two local hat bars offer a unique, hands-on experience where you can **design, decorate, and personalize** your hat with branding, burn designs, feathers, and accessories.

- **American Paint Hat Co—3820 Charlotte Ave (The Nations):** Located in the stylish **L&L Market**, this hat studio offers a **hands-on design experience**. It offers a selection of branded burns, hat bands, and custom accessories. Guests can work one-on-one with a hat specialist to craft a **fully customized hat** that suits their personality.

www.americanpainthat.com/

- **Rustler Hat Co—407 11th Ave S (The Gulch):** This **high-end hat boutique** specializes in premium, classic cowboy and western hats. It focuses on **traditional Western craftsmanship** and offers options to **steam-shape, distress, and burn** your hat to give it a **rugged, vintage look.** This location is ideal for serious hat lovers and collectors. www.rustlerhatco.com/

Goo Goo Cluster Chocolate Co. - 116 3rd Ave S: The downtown location offers a fun, interactive experience where visitors can **make their own custom Goo Goo Clusters**—Nashville's famous chocolate, caramel, and peanut candy. You can use the "Design Your Own Confection" station or participate in hands-on chocolate-making classes. https://googoo.com/pages/experience

Hatch Show Print - 224 Rep. John Lewis Way S: Established in **1879**, this working print shop has designed legendary **handmade posters for musicians, festivals, and events**, using traditional techniques that give each print its **signature vintage style** (*Home - Hatch Show Print*, 2024). Visitors can take a guided **tour of the shop**, learn about the history of letterpress printing, and even **create their own custom Hatch Show print** as a souvenir. The store also features a gallery and gift shop, where guests can purchase unique posters and Nashville-inspired artwork. www.hatchshowprint.com/

JoyRide Golf Cart Tours—833 9th Ave S: This company offers unique **golf cart tours** and an open-air experience to explore the city's landmarks, murals, and local hotspots. Tours operate daily, including **sightseeing adventures, mural and Instagram tours**, and **brewery/distillery visits.** https://joyrideus.com/nashville/

UNIQUE THINGS-TO-DO

Kayak Down the Cumberland River - 2 Victory Ave: River Queen Voyages offers an exceptional way to experience Nashville's scenic beauty through **kayak and pedal pontoon boat rentals** on the Cumberland River. **Rental Options:** RiverQueenVoyages.com

- **Skyline Route:** This popular 3-mile, one-hour paddle starts at Shelby Park and concludes downtown. It offers stunning views of Nashville's skyline and includes a complimentary shuttle to the launch point.
- **Out & Back Rental:** For a flexible adventure, opt for the 90-minute rental starting and ending at 2 Victory Ave. Paddle at your own pace, exploring the downtown riverfront.

Kung Fu Saloon - 1921 Division St: Vintage arcade bar with **FREE** skee ball 7 days a week, full bar, private karaoke rooms, and the largest patio in Midtown! 21+ https://kungfusaloon.com/locations/nashville/

Lip Lab - 5014 Broadway Place: This innovative store offers personalized experiences where clients can create their own custom lipstick shades. With the assistance of color experts, guests can mix their perfect hue, choose from various finishes such as matte, satin, sheer, balm, or gloss, add a preferred scent, and even personalize the packaging with custom engraving. www.liplab.com/

Mural Art Tour: Nashville is home to a **thriving street art scene** featuring colorful murals that make for Instagram-worthy photo opportunities. Visitors can explore these stunning works of art **on a guided tour or at their own pace.** www.visitmusiccity.com/nashville-trip-ideas/nashville-murals

- **GUIDED Mural Tours:** Several companies, like **Joyride Nashville** and **Nashville Mural Tours,** offer guided tours via **golf carts, vans, or private vehicles. These tours** take guests to the city's most iconic murals and provide insight into the artists and history behind each piece. They typically last **1-2 hours** and stop at famous locations like the **"I Believe in Nashville"** mural in 12 South, the **Gulch Wings** mural, and many hidden gems throughout the city.

- **SELF-GUIDED Mural Tour:** For those who prefer to explore at their own pace, visitors can **walk or drive** through popular neighborhoods like **The Gulch, 12 South, East Nashville, and Downtown**, where murals are abundant. Many travelers use online mural maps to locate must-see street art while stopping for coffee or local shopping along the way.

NashTrash Tours - 900 Rosa L. Parks: Famously known for their **Big Pink Bus.** This tour offers a comedic and entertaining journey through the city, highlighting its rich history and culture. The tour begins and ends in the Nashville Farmers Market parking lot. www.nashtrash.com/

Paddywax Candle Bar - 408 11th Ave S: A unique, hands-on experience where guests can **create their own custom candles**. Located in the Gulch neighborhood, this workshop allows participants to select their favorite vessel and fragrance and then follow a guided process to pour a personalized candle. The **self-guided, 45-minute sessions** are perfect for individuals or groups. Candles are ready for pickup three hours after pouring or can be shipped for an additional fee. Participants are also welcome to bring their own beer, wine, or seltzers for a small corkage fee. https://thecandlebar.co/

Pedal Taverns: A fun and energetic way to explore the city while enjoying drinks with friends. This **party on wheels,** operated by companies like **Nashville Pedal Tavern** and **Sprocket Rocket**, takes groups on a mobile bar tour through **Broadway, Midtown, and The Gulch**. Guests pedal their way between bars and iconic landmarks while a driver steers and a guide keeps the party going with music and games. /www.nashvillepedaltavern.com/ https://sprockettours.com/

Play Playground - 128 2nd Ave: This new two-story, 15,000 square-foot attraction features over **20 large-scale immersive games**, including physical challenges and nostalgic puzzles, designed to provide a socially competitive atmosphere (*Home | Play Playground Nashville*, n.d.). Guests can enjoy creative cocktails, mocktails from the bar, live music, and DJs. The venue also boasts a **rooftop space** with panoramic views of Nissan Stadium and the Cumberland River. www.playplayground.com/nashville/

Pub Crawl: Nashville offers various **pub crawls** catering to different interests. Take a guided walking tour through historic areas like 2nd Avenue and Printers Alley. Enjoy samples of local craft brews, specialty drinks, and Tennessee moonshines. **Here are some notable options:**

- **Music City Pub Crawl**: Nashville's original and longest-running pub crawl. www.musiccitypubcrawl.com/
- **The Ville Tours All-Inclusive Pub Crawl by Joyride Tours** - https://joyrideus.com/nashville-tn/the-ville-all-inclusive-pub-crawl/
- **Crawl Nashville** - https://crawlnashville.com/

Puttshack Nashville - 138 12th Ave N: Located in The Gulch, this high-tech mini-golf spot features four one-of-a-kind courses with Trackaball™ technology for automatic scoring and interactive play. But it's not just about the golf—Puttshack offers a globally inspired menu and a full bar, making it perfect for family outings, date nights, or hanging out with friends. Plus, the venue amps up the fun with live

DJs on weekends. www.puttshack.com/locations/nashville

Red Bus Tour: Offered through the **Old Town Trolley Tours**. This unlimited **hop-on, hop-off** experience features red and green trolleys, providing a comprehensive overview of the city's landmarks and attractions. The tour includes **13 stops**, allowing guests to explore sites such as the **Country Music Hall of Fame**, **Ryman Auditorium**, and **Centennial Park** at their own pace. The complete loop lasts approximately **90 minutes**, with trolleys arriving at each stop every **30 minutes** (Old Town Trolley Tours, n.d.). www.trolleytours.com/nashville/hop-on-hop-off

Rent Bikes and Electric Scooters: Explore **Downtown Nashville** at your own pace. Several companies, including **BCycle** for bike rentals and **Lime, Bird, and Spin** for electric scooters, offer convenient, app-based rentals throughout the city. Riders can **unlock a bike or scooter using a mobile app**, ride through popular areas like **Broadway, The Gulch, and Riverfront Park**, and **drop off their rental at designated locations** when finished. These rentals provide a fun, efficient, and eco-friendly way to navigate Music City. www.levyelectric.com/resources/your-guide-to-renting-electric-scooters-in-nashville%2C-tennessee

Shop for COWBOY BOOTS! The best way to buy cowboy boots while visiting Nashville is to explore the many boot stores downtown and in The Gulch, where you'll find everything from classic Western styles to trendy, fashion-forward designs. **Broadway** is home to well-known retailers like **Boot Barn, Big Time Boots, and French's Shoes & Boots**, offering a wide selection at various prices. **Lucchese Bootmaker in The Gulch** is a must-visit for luxury handcrafted boots, known for its high-quality leather and expert craftsmanship. Many stores also offer **"Buy One, Get Two Free"** deals, so it's worth checking multiple locations to find the best value. https://notesonnashville.com/things-to-do/shopping/nashville-cowboy-boots-buying-guide/

The Listening Room Cafe - 618 4th Ave S: A live music venue and restaurant in Nashville's SoBro neighborhood. This renowned destination offers an intimate setting where patrons can enjoy performances by up-and-coming and established hit songwriters. Using a "songwriters in the round" setup, guests will enjoy a unique opportunity to experience the stories behind the songs. www.listeningroomcafe.com/

The Nashville ZOO at Grassmere - 3777 Nolensville Pike: Spanning 188 acres, the zoo is home to over 6,000 animals representing 339 species, offering visitors the opportunity to explore diverse exhibits such as the **African Savannah, Expedition Peru,** and **Tiger Crossroads** (*Nashville Zoo at Grassmere | Nashville, TN*, n.d.). In addition to animal exhibits, the zoo features experiences like the **Kangaroo Kickabout, Lorikeet Landing,** and the **Soaring Eagle Zip Line**. The zoo operates year-round with seasonal hours and special events. www.nashvillezoo.org/

Topgolf Nashville - 500 Cowan St: A premier **golf entertainment venue** in **East Nashville**, offering a high-tech driving range, climate-controlled hitting bays, and interactive games for all skill levels. Guests can enjoy a full-service **restaurant and bar, rooftop terrace,** live music events, and golf. https://topgolf.com/us/nashville/

Walk Eat Nashville Food Tour: Experience a tasty, guided walking tour through some of Nashville's most vibrant neighborhoods. Along the way, you'll sample classic Southern dishes and discover hidden culinary gems, all while learning about the city's rich history, culture, and buzzing food scene. With stops at **locally loved restaurants, bakeries, and specialty shops**, this tour is perfect for foodies looking to experience authentic Nashville cuisine beyond the usual tourist hotspots. **Tours are offered in Downtown, East Nashville, and The Gulch. www.walkeatnashville.com**

Photo Credit: Sean Pavone

19

CHRISTMAS EVENTS & SHOWS

Experience the magic of the holiday season in Nashville with these festive activities.

A Country Christmas at Gaylord Opryland Resort: Bring the holiday spirit to life with a magical winter wonderland at Opryland Hotel and marvel at over three million holiday lights on display throughout the resort. Gaylord Opryland Christmas

- **ICE! featuring Frosty the Snowman:** Experience larger-than-life ice sculptures and displays depicting scenes from "Frosty the Snowman," all crafted from over two million pounds of ice (*Christmas at Gaylord Opryland*, n.d.).
- **A Country Christmas Dinner Show:** Enjoy a festive meal with live performances of classic and original holiday music and favorite country hits.
- **Ice Tubing and Ice Skating:** Participate in winter fun with ice tubing lanes and an ice skating rink suitable for all ages.

- **Gingerbread Decorating Corner:** Decorate gingerbread houses and cookies, a delightful activity for families and children.
- **Carriage Rides:** Take a scenic horse-drawn carriage ride around the resort's beautifully decorated grounds.

A Dickens of a Christmas in Franklin - Step back in time with this Victorian-era street festival in historic downtown Franklin, featuring costumed characters, carolers, and festive activities. https://williamsonheritage.org/events/dickens-of-a-christmas/

FrankTown Festival of Lights - Drive through a mile of over 200 synchronized light displays at the Williamson County Ag Expo Center in Franklin, about 30 miles south of Nashville. Walkin' Wednesdays offer a chance to explore on foot. https://franktownsfestivaloflights.com/

Holiday Concerts at the Ryman Auditorium - Catch special holiday performances at the historic Ryman Auditorium, where you can enjoy shows by famous artists and festive concerts that really capture the magic of the season. www.ryman.com/holidays

Holiday LIGHTS at Cheekwood Estate & Gardens - Stroll through the beautifully illuminated gardens adorned with over a million lights, visit the reindeer village and enjoy seasonal activities. https://cheekwood.org/calendar-events/holiday-lights/

Holiday Pop-Up Bars - Visit themed pop-up bars across Nashville offering festive cocktails and immersive holiday decorations, such as Camp Bobby at the Bobby Hotel and The Mistletoe Club at Eddie Ate Dynamite. https://nashvillelifestyles.com/nashville-calendar/things-to-do/holiday-pop-up-bars-in-nashville/

CHRISTMAS EVENTS & SHOWS

Nashville Christmas Parade - Join the annual downtown parade featuring festive floats, marching bands, and an appearance by Santa Claus, celebrating the holiday spirit with the community. https://nashvillechristmasparade.com/

Nashville's Nutcracker by Nashville Ballet - Experience the classic holiday ballet performed by the Nashville Ballet at the Tennessee Performing Arts Center, bringing Tchaikovsky's score to life with enchanting choreography and vibrant costumes. https://www.nashvilleballet.com/

Tennessee Performing Arts Center - Each year, **TPAC** hosts a variety of festive performances, from timeless classics like *A Christmas Carol* and *The Nutcracker* to family favorites like *A Charlie Brown Christmas Live on Stage*. www.tpac.org/events

The Dancing Lights of Christmas - Enjoy Tennessee's largest drive-thru light and music show at the Wilson County Fairgrounds, about 30 miles east of Nashville, featuring synchronized displays and a festive atmosphere. www.thedancinglightsofchristmas.com/

Zoolumination at Nashville Zoo (November - February) - Experience the zoo transformed into a wonderland with over a million lights and Asian-inspired lantern displays, including life-sized animals and mythical creatures. www.nashvillezoo.org/zoolumination

VI

GREEN SPACES & SPORTS

20

PARKS & OPEN GREEN SPACES

Enjoy nature, recreation, and cultural landmarks in one of these notable parks and open areas in and around the city.

Downtown

Bicentennial Capitol Mall State Park - 600 James Robertson Pkwy: A 19-acre historical park in the heart of **Downtown Nashville** and located near the **Tennessee State Capitol**, this park features **a 200-foot-wide granite map of Tennessee**, a **Pathway of History** with historical inscriptions and the impressive **Court of 95 Bell Carillon**, which rings melodies throughout the day (*Bicentennial Capitol Mall State Park*, n.d.). With wide open spaces, walking trails, and stunning views of the Capitol, the park is perfect for picnics, photography, and learning about the state's heritage. It's also home to the **Nashville Farmers' Market**, making it an **excellent stop for fresh food and local flavors.** https://tnstateparks.com/parks/bicentennial-mall

Centennial Park - 2500 West End Ave: One of Nashville's most beloved urban green spaces, offering **132 acres of scenic beauty, history, and recreation** (*Centennial Park*, n.d.). Located just west of downtown, this park is home to the **full-scale replica of the Parthenon**, one of the city's most iconic landmarks. Visitors can **stroll through walking trails, relax by the lake, enjoy open green spaces, and explore the beautiful sunken garden**. Centennial Park also hosts **concerts, art exhibits, and community events.** www.nashville.gov/departments/parks/parks/centennial-park

Cumberland Park - 592 South 1st Street: A **6.5-acre modern urban park** along the **east bank of the Cumberland River** adjacent to Nissan Stadium and next to the Shelby Street Pedestrian Bridge. The park offers innovative play spaces, including a climbing wall, water features, a splash pad, an outdoor amphitheater, and scenic views of the Cumberland River. (Great location for taking photos of Nashville's skyline.) https://nashvilledowntown.com/go/cumberland-park

Sevier Park - 3000 Granny White Pike: Located in the **12 South neighborhood**, this **20-acre urban park** offers open green spaces, walking paths, playgrounds, and a community center and hosts a weekly farmers' market, providing a community hub for locals and visitors. https://nashvilleguru.com/businesses/sevier-park

Shelby Park and Bottoms - 1900 Davidson St: A **1,300-acre urban green space** (larger than Central Park in NYC) located just minutes from downtown in **East Nashville**, offers a mix of recreation, nature, and scenic river views **along the Cumberland River**. A favorite among walkers, cyclists, and nature lovers, the park features paved and unpaved trails, playgrounds, sports fields, disc golf, a dog park, fishing areas, and two golf courses (*About the Park — Friends of Shelby Park*, n.d.). The **Shelby Bottoms Greenway & Natural Area** is home to **nearly 10**

miles of trails, wetlands, and diverse wildlife. Visitors can also stop by the **Shelby Bottoms Nature Center**, which offers **educational exhibits and environmental programs**. www.nashville.gov/departments/parks/nature-centers-and-natural-areas/shelby-bottoms-nature-center

Surrounding Areas

Beaman Park - 5911 Old Hickory Blvd: A **1,678-acre nature preserve** located **30 minutes north of Nashville**, offering a peaceful escape into the wilderness just a short drive from downtown (*Beaman Park*, n.d.). Known for its **rugged terrain, scenic hiking trails, and diverse plants and wildlife**, the park is a favorite among hikers, birdwatchers, and nature enthusiasts. Visitors can explore **miles of trails** winding through **hardwood forests, creeks, and ridges**. www.nashville.gov/departments/parks/nature-centers-and-natural-areas/beaman-park-nature-center

Bells Bend Park - 4187 Old Hickory Blvd: An **808-acre natural area** located **30 minutes northwest of Nashville** (*Bells Bend Park*, n.d.). Unlike many other parks in the city, Bells Bend is known for its **wide-open spaces and rolling meadows**, making it an excellent destination for **hiking, horseback riding, and wildlife observation**. The park features **several miles of trails**, including the **Bells Bend Loop Trail**, which provides stunning views of the **Cumberland River**. www.nashville.gov/departments/parks/nature-centers-and-natural-areas/bells-bend-outdoor-center/bells-bend-park

Edwin and Percy Warner Parks - 7311 TN-100: Collectively known as **Warner Parks**, these two adjoining parks cover over **3,100 acres about 30 minutes west of downtown Nashville**, offering extensive hiking trails, scenic roadways, paved biking and running paths, picnic areas, a dog park, mountain bike trails, equestrian paths, golf courses, and breathtaking scenic overlooks (*Warner Parks*, n.d.). They are **among the largest municipal parks in Tennessee**. Warner Parks provides a peaceful escape from the city, just a short drive from downtown. The parks are also home to the **Warner Park Nature Center**, which offers educational programs, and the historic **Steeplechase horse racing track**. www.nashville.gov/departments/parks/parks/warner-parks

Radnor Lake State Park - 1160 Otter Creek Rd: A **1,368-acre protected natural area** just **30 minutes south of Nashville**, offers a serene escape for hiking, wildlife viewing, and photography. This pristine park features **over 6 miles of scenic trails**, including the **Lake Trail**, which provides breathtaking views of Radnor Lake, and more challenging routes like **Ganier Ridge Trail** for those seeking elevation. Known for its rich biodiversity, visitors frequently spot **deer, otters, owls, bald eagles, and other native wildlife** in their natural habitat. **Swimming, fishing, and biking are prohibited** to maintain the park's peaceful environment, but **ranger-led programs and guided hikes** offer educational insights into the area's unique ecosystem (*Radnor Lake State Park*, n.d.). https://tnstateparks.com/parks/radnor-lake

21

SPORTS

Professional Sports

Tennessee Titans (NFL): Competing in the National Football League, they play their home games at **Nissan Stadium**. www.tennesseetitans.com/

Nashville Predators (NHL): This National Hockey League team brings excitement to the ice at **Bridgestone Arena**. www.bridgestonearena.com/teams/detail/predators

Nashville SC (MLS): As a Major League Soccer team, Nashville SC hosts matches at **GEODIS Park**. www.nashvillesc.com/

Nashville Sounds (MiLB): The city's Minor League Baseball team plays at **First Horizon Park**. www.milb.com/nashville

College Sports

Vanderbilt University Commodores: Vanderbilt participates in NCAA Division I athletics and field teams in football, basketball, baseball, and more. https://vucommodores.com/

Belmont University Bruins: Belmont competes in NCAA Division I and offers programs in basketball, soccer, and more. https://belmontbruins.com/

Tennessee State University Tigers: This institution's teams participate in NCAA Division I sports, including football and basketball. https://tsutigers.com/

Golf Courses

Two Rivers Golf Course - 2235 Two Rivers Pkwy: A scenic **18-hole public course** in **East Nashville** offers rolling fairways, challenging greens, and stunning views of the downtown skyline. This **par-72 course** is ideal for golfers of all skill levels. The facility also features a driving range, practice greens, and a pro shop. www.nashville.gov/departments/parks/golf-courses/two-rivers-golf-course

Harpeth Hills Golf Course - 2424 Old Hickory Blvd: This championship **18-hole public course,** tucked into the rolling hills of **Percy Warner Park in West Nashville**, offers a challenging layout with scenic fairways and well-kept greens. Whether you're a casual golfer or a seasoned pro, the **par-72 course** promises a rewarding experience for everyone. The course features elevation changes, water hazards, and tree-lined fairways, making it one of the region's most picturesque and competitive public courses. Additional amenities include a driving range, practice greens, and a pro shop. www.nashville.gov/departments/parks/golf-courses/harpeth-hills-golf-course

Percy Warner Golf Course - 1221 Forrest Park Dr: A scenic **9-hole public course** located within **Percy Warner Park** in **West Nashville**. This **par-34 course** offers a relaxed and enjoyable round of golf, perfect for beginners, casual players, or those looking for a quick game. With tree-lined fairways, gentle rolling hills, and a peaceful natural setting, Percy Warner Golf Course provides a **laid-back atmosphere** while still offering a few strategic challenges. www.nashville.gov/departments/parks/golf-courses/percy-warner-golf-course

Public Sports Complexes

Centennial Sportsplex - 222 25th Ave N: Nashville's premier multi-sport facility, offering **ice skating rinks, an Olympic-sized swimming pool, indoor and outdoor tennis courts, and a fitness center**. Located near **Centennial Park**. www.nashville.gov/departments/parks/centennial-sportsplex

E.S. Rose Park - 1000 Edgehill Ave: A 24-acre community sports complex in Nashville's **Edgehill neighborhood** featuring **baseball and softball fields, a soccer field, a basketball court, and a walking track**. Home to **Belmont University's athletic teams**, the park also welcomes the public for recreational activities and local events. www.belmont.edu/community/rose-park.html

22

Share Your Experience

Thank you for exploring **Nashville** with this travel guide! Whether planning your visit, currently experiencing Music City, or reflecting on your trip, I hope this guide has helped you **discover the best attractions, hidden gems, and local favorites** that make Nashville unique.

If you found this guide helpful, informative, and well-organized, I'd greatly appreciate it if you could take a moment to **leave a review**. Your feedback helps improve future editions and assists other travelers in finding the best resource to plan their time in Nashville.

This guide was designed to be **comprehensive and easy to navigate**, covering everything from **hotels and attractions to nightlife, dining, and unique experiences**. If it made your trip **smoother and more enjoyable or inspired you to explore something new**, I'd love to hear about it!

I appreciate your support and hope you have an unforgettable time in **Music City**! ♪

SHARE YOUR EXPERIENCE

* * *

*NOTE: If you'd like to suggest a business to be added to this travel guide or considered for future editions, we'd love to hear from you! Please email your recommendation to **401publishing@gmail.com** and include the business name, location, and any details that make it a great fit. Your input helps us create a more comprehensive and valuable resource for travelers.

Photo Credit: Jeremy Poland

QR Code to Leave a Review

23

Conclusion

I hope this guide has helped you discover the best of Music City—from its legendary music scene and vibrant nightlife to its beautiful parks, exciting sports, and unique local experiences.

This city constantly evolves, offering new attractions, festivals, and events throughout the year. No matter how often you visit, **there's always something new to explore**.

Thank you for using this travel guide—I hope it made your trip more manageable, exciting, and unforgettable. Until next time, keep the music playing and **enjoy your Nashville adventure!**

References

1 Hotels. (n.d.). *1 hotels*. https://www.1hotels.com/

About - Moto Cucina + Enoteca. (n.d.). Moto. https://www.motonashville.com/about

About the park — Friends of Shelby Park. (n.d.). Friends of Shelby Park. https://www.friendsofshelby.org/the-park

Adventure Science Center. (2025, January 29). *Home | Adventure Science Center*. https://adventuresci.org/

Auditorium, R. (n.d.). *Ryman Auditorium*. Ryman Auditorium. https://www.ryman.com/

Beaman Park. (n.d.). https://www.tn.gov/environment/program-areas/na-natural-areas/natural-areas-middle-region/middle-region/beaman-park.html

Before you continue to Google Maps. (n.d.). https://www.google.com/maps

Belle Meade Historic Site. (n.d.). *Belle Meade Historic site*. https://visitbellemeade.com/

Bells Bend Park. (n.d.). Nashville.gov. https://www.nashville.gov/departments/parks/nature-centers-and-natural-areas/bells-bend-outdoor-center/bells-bend-park

Belmont Mansion | Nashville Historic House Museum |. (n.d.). Belmont mansion. https://www.belmontmansion.com/

Bicentennial Capitol Mall State Park. (n.d.). Bicentennial Capitol Mall State Park. Retrieved February 8, 2025, from https://tnstateparks.com/parks/bicentennial-mall

Bowl, B. (n.d.). *Nashville | Brooklyn Bowl.* https://www.brooklynbowl.com/nashville

C H O P P E r. (n.d.). C H O P P E R. https://www.choppertiki.com/

Cannery Hall. (2023, November 13). *Home - Cannery Hall.* https://canneryhall.com/

Centennial Park. (n.d.). Nashville.gov. https://www.nashville.gov/departments/parks/parks/centennial-park

Christmas at Gaylord Opryland. (n.d.). Gaylord Opryland. Retrieved February 6, 2025, from https://christmasatgaylordopryland.marriott.com/

Corbin, M. (2021, November 12). Carne Mare, a Contemporary Italian Chophouse from Chef Andrew Carmellini, Opens in the Gulch. *Eater Nashville.* https://nashville.eater.com/2021/11/12/22776964/first-look-carne-mare-w-hotel-nashville-gulch-

REFERENCES

andrew-carmellini

Downtown Nashville - The Best Restaurants and Things to Do. (n.d.). Nashville Go. https://nashvillego.com/neighborhoods/downtown

Downtown Nashville Hotels Near Bridgestone Arena | Hotel Indigo® Nashville. (n.d.). IHG. https://www.ihg.com/hotelindigo/hotels/us/en/nashville/bnaus/hoteldetail?cm_mmc=GoogleMaps-_-IN-_-US-_-BNAUS

Downtown · Nashville, TN, USA. (n.d.). Downtown · Nashville, TN, USA. https://www.google.com/maps/place/Downtown,+Nashville,+TN/@36.1697893,-86.8180946,13z/data=!4m6!3m5!1s0x88646658bb4caa27:0x5df901d75c502b6f!8m2!3d36.1605094!4d-6.7784325!16s%2Fg%2F11b62rzxh8?entry=ttu&g_ep=EgoyMDI1MDIxMi4wIKXMDS0ASAFQAw%3D%3D

Eastside Bowl. (2023, December 1). *Eastside Bowl.* https://eastsidebowl.com/

Exit/In. (2023, March 14). *History - Exit/In | Nashville's Music Forum Since 1971.* Exit/in | Nashville's Music Forum Since 1971. https://exitin.com/about/

FOLK. (n.d.). FOLK. https://www.goodasfolk.com/

Geheren, M. (2022, June 28). *Conrad Nashville ushers in a new era of luxury to music City.* Stories From Hilton. https://stories.hilton.com/releases/conrad-nashville-opens

Germantown. (2023, October 9). Visit Nashville TN.

https://www.visitmusiccity.com/explore-nashville/ neighborhoods/germantown

Golf, party venue, sports bar & restaurant | TopGolf Nashville. (n.d.). Topgolf. https://topgolf.com/us/nashville/

Hgadmin. (2023, September 5). *Welcome to the Nashville International Airport*. Nashville International Airport | BNA. Retrieved December 12, 2023, from https://flynashville.com

Historic estate in Nashville | Cheekwood Estate & Gardens. (2025, January 27). Cheekwood. https://cheekwood.org/

Home. (n.d.). https://chauvetarts.com/

Home | Play Playground Nashville. (n.d.). https://www.playplayground.com/nashville

Home - Hatch Show print. (2024, December 13). Hatch Show Print. https://www.hatchshowprint.com/

Hotels in Nashville downtown | JW Marriott Nashville. (n.d.). https://www.marriott.com/en-us/hotels/bnajw-jw-marriott-nashville/overview/?scid=f2ae0541-1279-4f24-b197-a979c79310b0

Hyatt. (2024). *Holston House Nashville*. Hyatt.com. Retrieved January 21, 2024, from https://www.hyatt.com/en-US/hotel/tennessee/holston-house-nashville/bnaub

Jimmy Kelly's Steakhouse. (n.d.). *Jimmy Kelly’s Steak-*

REFERENCES

house | Nashville Steakhouse since 1934. Jimmy Kelly's Steakhouse. https://jimmykellys.com/

John Seigenthaler Pedestrian Bridge | Downtown Nashville. (n.d.). https://nashvilledowntown.com/go/shelby-street-pedestrian-bridge

Justus, J. (2023, November 11). *Review of The Catbird Seat | Nashville, Tennessee - AFAR*. AFAR Media. https://www.afar.com/places/the-catbird-seat-nashville

Kraft, M. (2023, November 13). *7 Bizarre Nashville traditions that make our city the absolute best*. OnlyInYourState®. https://www.onlyinyourstate.com/tennessee/nashville/bizarre-nashville-traditions/

Live it up in downtown Nashville. (n.d.). NashvilleDowntown.com. https://nashvilledowntown.com/

Loews Nashville Hotel near Vanderbilt u. (n.d.). Loews Hotels & Co. https://www.loewshotels.com/vanderbilt-hotel

Marathon Music Works. (2024, September 20). *Home - Marathon Music Works*. Marathon Music Works - Nashville, TN. https://www.marathonmusicworks.com/

Marathon Village. (n.d.). https://marathonvillage.net/

Musicians Corner | Nashville's free concert series. (n.d.). Musicians Corner. https://www.musicianscornernashville.com/

Nashville Go: your guide to music City. (n.d.). Nashville Go. https://nashvillego.com/

Nashville Guide. (n.d.). JeTy Vacations. https://www.jetyvacations.com/nashville-guide-573948779

Nashville Guru. (2025, February 8). *Nashville Guru | The best of Nashville | NashvilleGuru.com.* https://nashvilleguru.com/

Nashville River Cruises | General Jackson Showboat. (2023, April 17). General Jackson. https://generaljackson.com/

Nashville Symphony. (n.d.). https://www.nashvillesymphony.org/

Nashville Zoo at Grassmere | Nashville, TN. (n.d.). https://nashvillezoo.org/

Nashville's best Italian Restaurant | Giovanni Ristorante. (n.d.). Giovanni's Ristorante. https://giovanninashville.com/

National Museum of African American Music | Nashville, TN. (n.d.). https://www.nmaam.org/

Nelson's Green Brier Distillery | Nelson's Green Brier Distillery. (n.d.). https://greenbrierdistillery.com/

Old Town Trolley Tours. (n.d.). *Nashville Tours voted #1 Save up to 18% on Nashville Tours.* https://www.trolleytours.com/nashville

Printer's Alley in Nashville - A Local's Guide. (n.d.-a). Nashville Go. https://nashvillego.com/activities/guides/printers-alley-the-

REFERENCES

complete-guide

Radnor Lake State Park. (n.d.). Radnor Lake State Park. Retrieved February 8, 2025, from https://tnstateparks.com/parks/radnor-lake

Robert's Western World | Nashville's Undisputed Home of Traditional Country Music. (n.d.). https://robertswesternworld.com/

Rolf & Daughters-Nashville-Restaurant-50Best Discovery. (n.d.). 50B - Discovery. https://www.theworlds50best.com/discovery/Establishments/US/Nashville/Rolf-and-Daughters.html

Sambuca Nashville. (n.d.). Sambuca Nashville. https://www.sambucanashville.com/

SCOB in Nashville. (n.d.). SCOB in Nashville. https://www.ilovesupperclub.com/

Sheraton Grand Nashville Downtown | Upscale stay in Nashville. (n.d.). https://www.marriott.com/en-us/hotels/bnand-sheraton-grand-nashville-downtown/overview/?scid=f2ae0541-1279-4f24-b197-a979c79310b0

Snellings, A. (2023, March 21). 15 Nashville slang terms you should know. *Mental Floss*. https://www.mentalfloss.com/posts/nashville-slang-terms

State Capitol | Tennessee State Museum. (n.d.). https://tnmuseum.org/state-capitol

Stoney River. (2023, November 10). *Best steakhouse in Nashville - Stoney*

River. https://stoneyriver.com/3015-west-end-avenue/

Tennessean, J. W. O. L. R. (2017, February 15). 30 Nashville phrases you should know. *The Tennessean.* https://www.tennessean.com/story/life/entertainment/12th/2017/02/15/30-nashville-phrases-you-should-know/97894602/

The Bowery Vault. (n.d.). The Bowery Vault. https://theboweryvault.com/

The Gulch. (2023, November 3). Visit Nashville TN. https://www.visitmusiccity.com/explore-nashville/neighborhoods/gulch#:~:text=The%20exceedingly%20walkable%20LEED%2Dcertified,traditional%20ramen%2C%20and%20Indian%20food.

The Gulch Nashville Hotels | W Nashville. (n.d.). https://www.marriott.com/en-us/hotels/bnawn-w-nashville/overview/

The Parthenon | Nashville's full-scale replica of the Greek landmark. (n.d.). The Parthenon. https://www.nashvilleparthenon.com/

The Treehouse. (n.d.). The Treehouse. https://treehousenashville.com/

Travel tips. (2022, June 7). Visit Nashville TN. https://www.visitmusiccity.com/plan-a-trip-to-nashville/travel-resources/travel-tips

UP Rooftop Table and Tavern | Official site. (n.d.). Up Rooftop. https://www.uprooftoplounge.com/

U.S. News & World Report. (2023, December 8). *15 Best Hotels in*

Downtown Nashville, Nashville | U.S. News Travel. https://travel.usnews.com/hotels/nashville_tn/n-downtown-nashville/

Visitors. (2023, March 7). Visit Nashville TN. https://www.visitmusiccity.com/

Von Elrod's Beer Hall & Kitchen. (2023, December 26). *Von Elrod's Beer Hall & Kitchen | Nashville, Tennessee.* https://vonelrods.com/

Warner Parks. (n.d.). Nashville.gov. https://www.nashville.gov/departments/parks/parks/warner-parks

Wikipedia contributors. (2024, August 26). *Gaylord Opryland Resort & Convention Center.* Wikipedia. https://en.wikipedia.org/wiki/Gaylord_Opryland_Resort_%26_Convention_Center

COVER Photo Credit: Sean Pavone

Also by Kelly Lee Culbreth

Kelly Lee Culbreth is an author known for her engaging and informative works that cater to both children and adults. Her publications include "Everything On The Farm Poops," an educational children's book that uses humor to teach about farm life, and "101 Fun Facts About Nashville, TN," a guide that offers readers a deeper appreciation for Music City's rich history and culture. Culbreth's books are both entertaining and educational for a wide audience.

101 Fun Facts About Nashville, TN

Discovering Music City One Fascinating Story at a Time!

In FULL COLOR!

Inside are 101 reasons why Nashville, TN has become one of the fastest-growing cities in America and one of the hottest tourist destinations in the world. With carefully selected facts, quirky stories, and numerous topics covered, even a local to Nashville will surely learn something new.

Everything On The Farm Poops at Christmas Coloring Book
Laugh-Out-Loud Designs and Silly Jokes
Featuring Festive Barn Animals, Santa's Crew, and Poop-Packed Holiday Fun.

🌲 **Deck the Stalls with Boughs of... Poop?** 🌲

This holiday season, get ready to embark on a side-splitting, color-filled adventure with the Everything On The Farm Poops at Christmas Coloring Book! Perfect for kids and adults alike, this uproarious collection of festive farmyard scenes is guaranteed to bring joy, laughter, and a touch of the unexpected to your holiday celebrations.

Everything On The Farm Poops
A #2 Best Seller!

HYSTERICAL, FUN, RHYMING BOOK!

Kids everywhere are fascinated with the farm and think poop is funny! This book will take you on a visit to the farm and show you all of its stinky charm. **But that stinky stuff has a purpose. Because without it, the garden and crops won't grow.** Filled with farm stories and educational humor that parents and kids will both enjoy.

Poop On The Potato Farm

A Story About Using Tractors, Poop Spreaders, Semi Trucks, and Other Farm Equipment to Turn Poop Into Money.

Holy cow, this farm has no dung! How do they grow those taters so big?!

Packed with farming facts, funny illustrations, and sidesplitting antics, kids will love this story about why nutrient-full manure is crucial to supplying America's essential foods. With a trip to the local dairy producer and learning about how natural fertilizer is collected and distributed, your children will become true excrement experts!

Poop On The Farm Compilation - 2 BOOKS IN 1!

Learn How an Illinois Farm and an Idaho Potato Farm Use Tractors, Farm Equipment, and Cow Poop to Grow Our Food.

Get both books in this convenient compilation!

Full of fun, colorful illustrations that include: cows, pigs, horses, goats, dogs, cats, tractors, poop spreaders, semi-trucks, compost turners, skid steers, and LOTS OF POOP.

Hotel Notes:

Restaurant Planning:

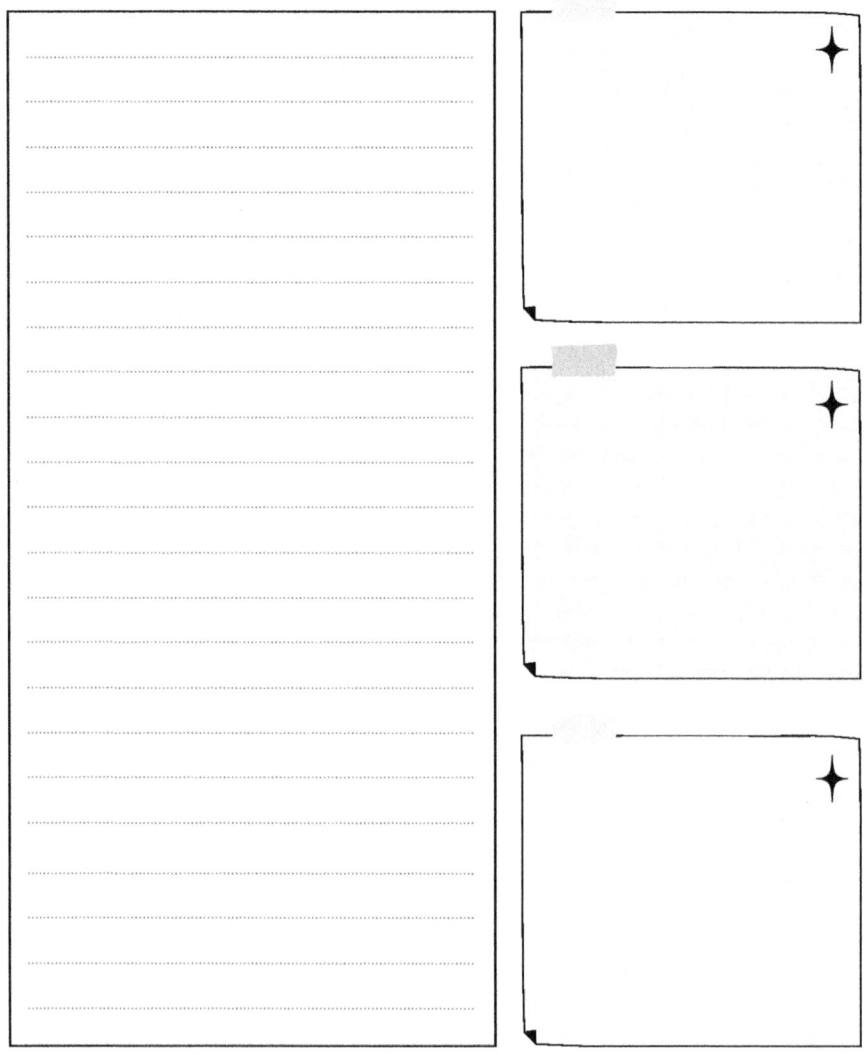

Live Music Venues:

Things-To-Do

Must See Attractions:

Concerts, Shows, & Events:

Notes:

Printed in Great Britain
by Amazon